George Stella's
Good Carb
Family Cookbook

Fast, Fun and Fresh Recipes...
Stella Style!

George Stella
with Christian Stella

Published By:
Dynamic Housewares Inc
20 West Bells Mill Road
Philadelphia, PA 19118

First Dynamic Housewares Inc paperback edition 2009

For information about special discounts for bulk purchases
please contact Dynamic Housewares Inc at:
sales@dynamichousewares.com

Please consult your physician before starting this or any other diet,
exercise, or lifestyle change program.

Authors: George Stella and Christian Stella
Cover, author and food photographs: Christian Stella
Archive and family photographs: Rachel Stella
Illustrations: Elise Stella
Book design and layout: Christian Stella

Manufactured in Canada

ISBN 978-1-60725-683-0

Acknowledgements

First and foremost, my family must express our deepest heartfelt thanks to our friends at Dynamic Housewares, who recognized something in me and actually published this book!

We would also like to thank Dr. Timothy O'Leary and his wife Kathleen until the day we can return their generosity. They believed in Rachel and me waaay back in the beginning and supported our cause to help make everything we do today possible; we will never forget that ever!

We would like to thank the friends that have become near and dear to our hearts. Friends like Dr. Frank Campisi of Campisi Health Centers in Orlando, FL, who helped not only my family but others every single day. Mary Beth and Michael Guard who entertained me for a weekend in their "Spa" guest house in Oklahoma City and have continued to unselfishly offer themselves and their expertise to help us in times of need.

Thank you to the Association of Junior League's International (www.ajli.org) for allowing me a platform to empower youth to make healthier food choices through hands on activities as spokesperson for the Junior League's Kids in the Kitchen initiative.

I dedicate this labor of love to my whole family who constructed it with great care, imparting pieces of themselves on every page in hopes to motivate and inspire others to eat healthier and live their lives to the fullest. To my son Christian and daughter in-law Elise, who did it ALL— designing the entire look of the book, taking all the photographs, drawing all of the illustrations—without them, this book would be nothing but pen on white paper. To my wife Rachel, who invented all the new recipes, shopped, cooked and styled all the food pics with me! I thank my lucky stars every day for my beautiful wife, who after 28 years, no matter how steep the hill, continues to walk side by side with me. I love her with all my heart and she has surely saved my life.

contents

contents
cont'd

introduction

The Good Life

The table is set and my whole family is gathered around. Four plates and four bowls in front of us, Rachel grabs the salad tongs. We've prepared a huge bowl of spring salad mix with roasted red peppers and cucumbers. Rachel made some Cajun blackened salmon for her salad and Christian went with chicken. On the side, Anthony made a quick stir-fry just because. All this food, it all looks so good—so very perfect—your eyes don't want to dig into and ruin it, but your stomach can hardly control itself.

Christian is raising his bowl.

Anthony's hand is on his fork.

Rachel's salad tongs are hovering just above this big bowl of beautiful salad.

And in my ear, in the little ear piece they're saying, "Don't touch the food. Fifteen more seconds. Go on! Dig in! But do not touch the food; we still need to film some close-ups!"

We all hold our hungry positions, unsure of what to do now. We take sips of water. Make some jokes and laugh. We say, "Hey, I'm still holding my fork up like I'm about to eat something. It's been up here a long time now, hasn't it?" The credits are rolling right along. It's just like any normal Stella family meal, minus the eating, or real walls around us. Then finally

the director calls CUT.

I pull the ear piece out of my ear and get to cooking some of the swap outs we'd hide under the counter during filming. The whole crew will be eating with my family today! I throw some chicken on the indoor grill and I look up into the lights. Mario, Emeril, Flay… they've all cooked on this stage. So how did *I* get here?

My name is George Stella and things were not always this way.

The Exact Opposite

Eight years ago, the scene around the Stella family dinner table was far bleaker. The food on the table was a stack of pizza boxes. There was a recycling bin under the table to throw the empty soda cans and bottles. And there was us. Over twelve hundred pounds of us.

Inside the house, I mostly wheeled myself around in this great big captain's chair I found on the side of the road. It was more comfortable than the wheelchair I used on my seldom trips outside. At 470 pounds, a doctor had told me that I was going to die.

My wife Rachel found herself over two hundred pounds, my son Anthony pushing 230. My younger son Christian was over 300 at only fifteen years old. I would be the first to die, for sure—but around this dinner table—it was clear to see that I was taking my whole family down with me.

Twenty years before, when I married Rachel, I was a professional chef cooking and innovating in some of South Florida's best restaurants. It's hard to pinpoint exactly how our lives, the lives of my whole family spiraled so far out of our control. On disability with heart failure, sleep apnea and a whole family on their way to diabetes, I had no idea where to

Anthony on his way to 220

Christian at 300 lbs

George at 470

Rachel over 200 lbs

3 1833 05545 6385

begin.

I've told this story so many times and it's always been important for me to mention that *Dr. Atkins New Diet Revolution* (and my wife!) saved our lives. If Rachel had not read the book from cover to cover and convinced the rest of the family that it was worth a try, I don't know where I'd be today. It was the exact opposite of what we thought we had to do to lose weight, but when you can't walk and you can't work and you can barely even breathe… well, you don't have much else to lose, no pun intended.

Find Your Style

I am a firm believer that if you want to lose weight, if you're really ready to lose weight, you can. Regardless of what you call the way you eat, you can lose weight if you eat fresh, healthy food. My family doesn't like to say that we've lost weight on the Atkins Diet or any other diet for that matter because after the first few months we didn't follow any one thing in particular. We lost our weight eating Stella Style—which is to say, our very own way.

And did we ever lose weight! The four of us lost over 560 pounds as a family and never looked back. Rachel and Anthony both dropped over 70 pounds. Christian lost more than half his weight going from 305 to under 150 and I did away with the 265 pounds that would have surely been the death of me. It wasn't an instant transformation, but it was as close to instant as I could imagine. I was dying at the dining room table one day, then two years later I was back in a restaurant kitchen a new man and chef.

Stella Style for us, was just a lifestyle switch. It was a decision to bypass processed, packaged foods that are generally unhealthy and instead eat

only fresh foods from the outer aisles of the grocery store. It was a decision to get back into the kitchen and cook for ourselves and to take pride in what we cook. Today most diets and weight loss plans have slowly found their way to this idea so I guess we were on to something, but I cannot stress this enough—find YOUR style and you'll surely be successful.

The Good, the Bad and the Carbohydrate

By now, I am sure that you've heard that all carbohydrates are not created equal. The swiftly digested—refined, processed, smashed, bleached, manufactured and who knows what else—"white" carbs have little nutritional value and turn straight into sugar, then fat in your body. These bad carbs are things like white flour, white rice, potatoes, sugar and all of the things made from them. Bad foods made from these bad carbs are everywhere you look; from soda to white bread, pastries, pasta, pizza and candy.

If you're in the mood for something starchy or sweet, you're not up the river without a paddle. There are plenty of good choices, good carbs out there for you. The carbohydrates in these foods are more complex, with more natural fiber. Fiber is key. The fiber helps you digest the carbohydrates slower, allowing you to burn them off before they're converted into sugar and then fat in your body. Just a few wholesome carbohydrates are whole wheat, whole oats, most fruits like berries and apples, vegetables, beans and even sweet potatoes. Not only will these good carbs keep you full and satisfied, they also pack more vitamins, minerals and antioxidants that you simply won't find in a refined, bad carb counterpart.

Lately, "whole grain" has started a good carb revolution for those who want to have their cake and eat it too. We're seeing more and more whole grains touted on advertisements, food packages and restaurant menus, but it's important to see the difference between good marketing and good food. While it's true that there are more and more whole grain foods to be found, always check the ingredients because something can still be whole grain and loaded with added sugars and partially hydrogenated oils, the dreaded trans-fat. What I mean is, just because it's whole grain, that doesn't mean the whole ingredient list is all that great!

Still not sure if it's up to snuff? A good whole grain food should have at least three grams of fiber per serving and if it doesn't, move right along.

Down With Counting

One of the biggest downfalls I've seen with people watching carbohydrates is the urge to count them out. Because all carbs—or even foods for that matter—are not created equal, you can't always go by the numbers.

For most of my weight loss I would say to myself that I was sticking to under 30 carbs a day—so even I was shackled to the numbers—but I realize now that I never kept a log of how many carbohydrates I was actually consuming. I was pretty sure that I was sticking to my goal carbs because I only kept fresh and good foods around the house. Today, I realize that my success had a whole lot to do with the good, fresh food and nothing to do with any arbitrarily derived carbohydrate limit.

When you're actively counting carbohydrates, or even calories, I believe you may inadvertently do more harm than good. You may find yourself eating *more* to reach just below your limit, just because you're allowed. Worse yet, you may find yourself saving up all of your carbs or calories for a food you probably shouldn't be eating in the first place. Starving yourself all day so that you can order a pizza and still stay below your daily carb limit isn't going to work out for you in the long run. A small chocolate candy may have the same amount of carbohydrates as a cup of broccoli, but these foods are so fundamentally different that it makes counting seem inane.

I've included nutritional information and carbohydrate counts on the recipes in this book, but remember that it's all about the food. My family and I have been eating these recipes, with great results, for years before we had to compile the counts for this book.

I say, throw the numbers out the window and make the choice to only eat good, fresh foods. It's a tough thing to let go, but it's probably best for your sanity as well! You can't live your whole life by the numbers… or at least I can't!

Your Own Family Cookbook

This book, my family's cookbook, is filled with the recipes of our success. These are the exact foods, the exact recipes we ate through our incredible weight loss and continue to eat years later.

It is our hope that our family can inspire you to enjoy good food as much as we do, to find the joys in cooking as we have and maybe even create your own family cookbook one day.

breakfast

APPLE WALNUT PANCAKES

CHILE RELLENOS HUEVOS

SHRIMPLY DELICIOUS FRITTATA

QUICK AND EASY CRÊPES

MUSHROOM SWISS MUFFIN CUP OMELETS

SAUSAGE, SAGE AND CHEESY
EGG CASSEROLE

BLUEBERRY BREAKFAST PAN BREAD

CHEESE BURRITO OMELET WRAPS

DAVID'S BREAKFAST SKILLET

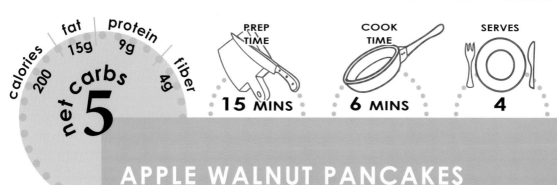

calories 200 | fat 15g | protein 9g | fiber 4g | net carbs 5

PREP TIME **15** MINS

COOK TIME **6** MINS

SERVES **4**

APPLE WALNUT PANCAKES

For some reason breakfast seems to be the one meal that people have trouble keeping exciting. Even I fall into the ho-hum fried egg routine at times and that's why we came up with a flour and sugar-free pancake mix. Because you can never really have too much of a good thing, we've made this tasty variation on our classic pancake recipe. Plus, the apples will keep doctors from coming into your kitchen and eating your lunch out of the fridge.

directions

1. Mix all the batter ingredients in a bowl with a rubber spatula or kitchen spoon until well blended and then scrape into a large measuring cup.

2. In a separate bowl mix together the filling ingredients.

3. Grease a griddle or nonstick pan with vegetable spray or butter and heat over medium heat for 2 minutes.

4. Pour 8 medium size cakes onto the hot griddle or pan and let cook on one side for 2 minutes. Before flipping, sprinkle each cake evenly with the filling and let cook for about 2 minutes more until golden brown on the bottom. Then flip the cakes and cook for about 2 minutes more to finish. Serve topped with a pat of butter and garnished with fresh apple slices if desired! Do I dare recommend sugar-free whipped cream? You bet I do!

shopping list 🖉

vegetable oil spray
BATTER
2 large eggs
1/4 cup water
1 tablespoon vanilla extract
1/2 cup almond flour
1/4 cup milled flax seed
1/4 cup sugar substitute (recommended: Splenda)
1 teaspoon baking powder
1/8 teaspoon salt
FILLING
1/4 teaspoon cinnamon
1/4 cup sugar substitute
1/2 cup fresh diced apple
1/4 cup coarse chopped walnuts
SPECIAL EQUIPMENT: griddle or large nonstick pan

GEORGE'S TIPS:

Make sure to have the griddle heated up and do not turn the pancakes over too soon; take a peek at the bottom and if it comes up easily and looks golden brown go ahead and flip 'em!

Watching cholesterol? Eggbeaters or egg whites may be used in place of whole eggs.

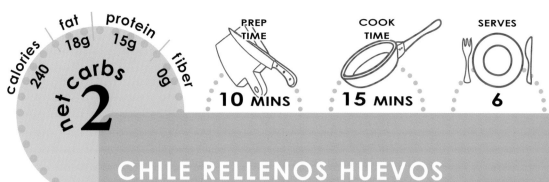

calories **240** | fat **18g** | protein **15g** | fiber **0g** | net carbs **2**

PREP TIME **10 MINS** | COOK TIME **15 MINS** | SERVES **6**

breakfast

CHILE RELLENOS HUEVOS

I have been surrounded by ethnic diversity in kitchens my entire life. From French and Haitian to Cuban and Mexican foods, I love them ALL. Two big favorites of mine have always been Chile Rellenos or baked stuffed green chili peppers and Huevos Rancheros a spicy scramble with salsa and chorizo. This easy to make combination of the two has a snazzy presentation and will have everyone shouting Ole'! I promise that they're easier to make than pronounce!

shopping list

vegetable oil spray
4 ounces chorizo sausage, cooked and diced (may use any breakfast sausage)
6 large eggs
4 ounces diced green chile peppers (canned preferred)
1/2 cup grated cheddar cheese
1/2 cup grated Monterey jack cheese
SPECIAL EQUIPMENT: 6 cup nonstick or silicone muffin pan

directions

1. Place rack in the center position and preheat the oven to 375 degrees F.

2. Spray the muffin pan with vegetable oil and divide the cooked diced chorizo equally into each of the six cups.

3. Crack an egg into each of the cups over the sausage, trying to keep the yolks unbroken and bake for about 12-14 minutes until the egg whites are cooked.

4. Remove the pan from the oven and top each cooked egg with equal amounts of chili peppers and both types of cheese and place back into the oven for just 1 minute more until the cheese is melted. Remove.

5. Let the eggs stand in the muffin pan for 2 minutes to set before removing each egg with a small rubber spatula or fork to serve. (They should hold together like a muffin) Serve topped with a dollop of sour cream and salsa if desired. Goes great with guacamole or a slice of fresh avocado as well!

GEORGE'S TIPS:

Egg whites or Eggbeaters may be used in place of whole eggs to lower the cholesterol in this recipe. Turkey or soy breakfast sausage is a lower fat choice to use in place of the chorizo to lighten things up as well. Try halving the amount of cheese or using low-fat cheese to go even healthier still!

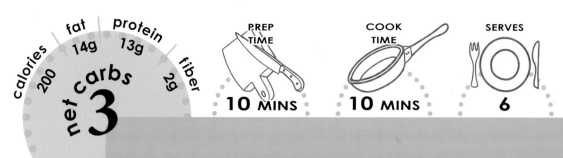

calories 200 | fat 14g | protein 13g | fiber 2g

net carbs **3**

PREP TIME **10 MINS**

COOK TIME **10 MINS**

SERVES **6**

breakfast

SHRIMPLY DELICIOUS FRITTATA

You say Frittata and I say, you gotta'… live it up once and a while that is! This scrumptious, easy cheesy shrimp breakfast pie is a sure-fire way to wake up your appetite. Bet those are five words you never thought you'd see together: easy, cheesy, shrimp, breakfast, pie. You just have to take the plunge on this one!

directions

1. Preheat the broiler and arrange the oven rack in the highest position.

2. Put the eggs, soy milk, salt and pepper in a bowl and whisk until frothy.

3. Place the oil in the skillet over medium-high heat, add the onion, garlic and shrimp and cook for about 2 minutes until shrimp are opaque.

4. With the pan still over the heat pour in the beaten eggs and let sit until the bottom starts to cook. Using a rubber spatula, slowly push the cooked egg from one side of the skillet to the other, allowing any raw egg to reach the bottom and cook; this also helps make the omelet fluffy and keeps the bottom from burning.

shopping list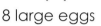

8 large eggs
1/4 cup unsweetened soy milk, (Silk brand recommended) may use water
1/4 teaspoon kosher salt
1/8 teaspoon freshly ground black pepper
2 tablespoons extra virgin olive oil
2 tablespoons sliced green onion tops
1 small garlic clove, minced
6 large shrimp, peeled, deviened and cut in half lengthwise
1 tablespoon fresh Italian parsley, stemmed and chopped
1/2 cup shredded Swiss cheese
1/2 cup marinated artichoke hearts, drained well and quartered
1/4 cup roasted red peppers, diced
1 lemon, cut into 6 wedges for garnish –optional
2 tablespoons sour cream for garnish - optional
SPECIAL EQUIPMENT: non-stick and oven safe pan, 10 or 12 inch

5. When the frittata is cooked on the bottom and the top is still runny, place the pan just under the broiler with the handle sticking out and the oven door open and broil for a minute or two until the eggs rise and start to brown.

6. Remove from under the broiler and scatter the cheese, artichokes and roasted peppers over the top of the frittata. Broil again for about 45 seconds to melt the cheese. Serve immediately, cut into 6 wedges, garnished with a dollop of sour cream, a sprig of parsley and a lemon wedge on the side if desired!

PREP TIME	COOK TIME	SERVES
10 MINS	8 MINS	4

calories 120 | fat 9g | protein 6g | fiber 0g

net carbs **3**

QUICK AND EASY CRÊPES

These flourless crêpes are a quick and easy delight that will brighten up any breakfast, hitting the spot when you are craving a decadent and delightful dessert! They are so rich that they've kept me out of the local pancake house while still keeping my sanity. Who needs all that sugar on the brain anyway?

directions

1. Add all crêpe shell ingredients, except butter, to a bowl and mix well with a whisk.

2. In a separate bowl, mix filling ingredients together with a fork until blended and set aside.

3. Melt about a teaspoon of the butter in an 8 inch non-stick pan over medium heat.

shopping list

CREPE SHELL
1/4 cup whole milk ricotta cheese
2 eggs
2 tablespoons sugar substitute (recommended: Splenda)
1 teaspoon cinnamon
1/2 teaspoon vanilla extract (no sugar added)
2 tablespoons butter or trans-fat free margarine

FILLING
1/4 cup whole milk ricotta cheese
2 tablespoons sugar substitute
1/4 teaspoon almond extract
1/2 cup fresh mixed berries, (optional)

4. Drop 2 heaping tablespoons of the crêpe mix in the hot pan and immediately tilt the pan back and forth to help spread the mix thinly, to the size of the pan.

5. Cook for only a minute or two until set and carefully flip the crêpe and cook for just another minute. Repeat this procedure until the mix is gone.

6. Fill each crêpe with around 1 heaping tablespoon of the filling and berries if you would like and roll up loosely. Garnish with some berries around the plate and top with homemade, no sugar whipped cream if desired!

 GEORGE'S TIPS:

Crêpe shells may be wrapped with wax or parchment paper in between and then kept fresh refrigerated or frozen in a zipper-lock bag.

calories **115**
fat **7.5g**
protein **10g**
fiber **0g**
net carbs **2**

PREP TIME
10 MINS

COOK TIME
15 MINS

SERVES
6

breakfast

MUSHROOM SWISS MUFFIN CUP OMELETS

I am a big fan of one pan meals and I make a ton of them for dinner; what's better than throwing everything in a pan or pot and taking it easy while the food cooks itself? Most recently I have been trying my hand at easy 1-step meals for breakfast. Well, nothing could be easier than this new rendition of a comforting mushroom Swiss omelet. It looks like a muffin, tastes like an omelet and practically makes itself!

shopping list

8 ounces sliced button mushrooms
6 large eggs
1/8 teaspoon kosher salt
1/8 teaspoon freshly ground black pepper
1/2 cup grated Swiss cheese (may use any cheese)
SPECIAL EQUIPMENT: 6 cup nonstick or silicone muffin pan

directions

1. Place the rack in the center position and preheat the oven to 375 degrees F.

2. Spray the muffin pan with vegetable oil and divide the sliced mushrooms equally into each of the six cups.

3. Crack an egg into each of the cups over the mushrooms and season evenly with the salt and pepper. Top each egg with equal amounts of cheese and bake for about 12-14 minutes until the whites are cooked but the yolks are still soft.

4. Remove the pan from the oven and let the eggs stand in the muffin pan for 2 minutes to set before removing each with a small rubber spatula or fork to serve. (They should hold together like a muffin) Serve hot.

 ## GEORGE'S TIPS:

Egg whites or Eggbeaters may be used in place of whole eggs to lower the cholesterol in this recipe. Try halving the amount of cheese or using low-fat cheese to go even healthier still!

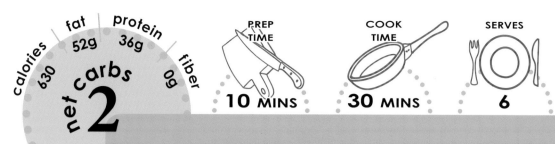

calories 630 · fat 52g · protein 36g · fiber 0g · net carbs **2**

PREP TIME **10 MINS** · COOK TIME **30 MINS** · SERVES **6**

breakfast

SAUSAGE, SAGE AND CHEESY EGG CASSEROLE

Serving six people (or 4 hungry ones!) for breakfast can be a hassle and that's why I like any recipe like this one that allows me to throw all the ingredients into a dish, bake and enjoy my coffee instead of flipping eggs.

directions

1. Place the rack in the center position and preheat the oven to 375 degrees F.

2. Spray the casserole dish with vegetable oil and layer the bottom with the cooked diced sausage and onion.

3. Crack the eggs into a bowl with all the remaining ingredients, mix well and pour over the sausage. Bake for 15 minutes or until the eggs are cooked through.

4. Remove from the oven and let the casserole cool for a few minutes to set before slicing into 6 servings. Remove each portion with a small spatula or fork and serve garnished with fresh sage leaves.

shopping list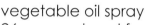

vegetable oil spray
26 ounces breakfast sausage, cooked and diced
1 tablespoon chopped red onion
6 large eggs
1/2 cup grated cheddar cheese
1/2 cup grated Monterey jack cheese
1/4 cup unsweetened soy milk (Silk brand recommended, may substitute half and half or cream)
4 ounces cream cheese, cut into small pieces
1/4 cup diced tomatoes (may use canned but drain well)
2 tablespoons chopped green bell pepper
1 teaspoon chopped fresh sage leaves (may use basil, cilantro or parsley)
1/4 teaspoon kosher salt
1/4 teaspoon freshly ground black pepper
1/8 teaspoon garlic powder
SPECIAL EQUIPMENT: 8 x 6 inch oven proof glass baking dish or pie pan

GEORGE'S TIPS:

Egg whites or Eggbeaters may be used in place of whole eggs to lower the cholesterol in this recipe. Turkey or soy breakfast sausage is a great way to lighten things up as well. Halving the amount of cheese or using low-fat cheeses is another way to slim this down.

Garnish with a dollop of fat-free sour cream for a guiltless twist!

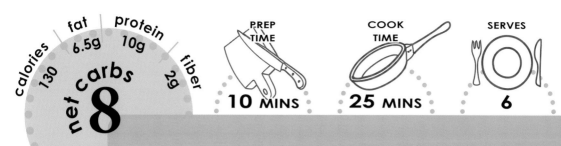

calories 130 | fat 6.5g | protein 10g | fiber 2g

net carbs **8**

PREP TIME 10 MINS

COOK TIME 25 MINS

SERVES 6

breakfast

BLUEBERRY BREAKFAST PAN BREAD

Breakfast can get real boring real fast, especially when trying to avoid choices like donuts or sugar filled muffins that stare us in the face at every corner. This easy to make gluten and sugar-free pan bread fills the void perfectly. It's not only good for you but instantly adds excitement to any meal or makes a great accompaniment to that first cup of morning java!

directions

1. Preheat the oven to 375 degrees F.

2. Spray the fry pan with the cooking spray. In a small bowl, mix together the 1 tablespoon soy flour and the 1/2 tablespoon sugar substitute. Evenly sprinkle the pan with the mixture, being careful to coat the sides by tilting the pan over the bowl to catch the crumbs.

shopping list

vegetable oil spray
1 cup plus 1 tablespoon soy flour
1/2 cup plus 1/2 tablespoon sugar substitute (recommended: Splenda)
1 1/2 teaspoons baking powder
2 large eggs
1/2 cup heavy cream (may use unsweetened soy milk)
1/3 cup club soda
1 teaspoon vanilla extract
1 tablespoon fresh ginger, peeled, minced and sprinkled with a teaspoon of sugar substitute
1/2 cup fresh blueberries (may use frozen)
SPECIAL EQUIPMENT: 8 inch oven proof frying pan (may use 6 cup muffin tin)

3. In a larger bowl whisk together the 1 cup soy flour, sugar substitute and baking powder. Add the eggs, heavy cream, club soda, vanilla and sweetened minced ginger and continue to whisk until completely blended.

4. Fold in the blueberries, pour the batter into the prepared pan and bake for about 25 minutes until the top starts to brown. The pan bread is done when lightly browned and a toothpick inserted in the center comes out clean.

5. Remove the pan from the oven and let cool for at least 5 minutes. Carefully loosen the bread around the edges with a spatula, cut into 6 pieces and serve warm with a pat of butter or low-fat cream cheese!

GEORGE'S TIPS:

Frozen blueberries work just fine for this recipe but use them frozen right into the batter. If thawed they will fall apart and turn the bread completely blue.

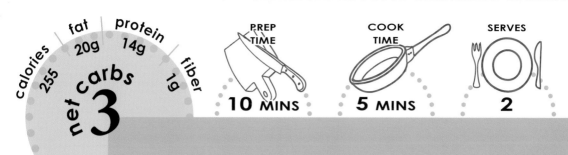

calories **255** · fat **20g** · protein **14g** · fiber **1g** · net carbs **3**

PREP TIME **10 MINS** · COOK TIME **5 MINS** · SERVES **2**

CHEESE BURRITO OMELET WRAPS

My first job as a chef was in a fast food Mexican restaurant when I was fifteen years old and one of my favorite things to make for myself was a cheese burrito! Maybe it was because I knew what went into the beef mixture but mostly because they were sooo easy and quick to make that I could eat them on the run. Although made from eggs these wraps have all the same ingredients and flavors I loved then and still love today without all the useless simple white carbs found in a flour tortilla.

shopping list

2 large eggs
2 tablespoons water
1/8 teaspoon salt
1/8 teaspoon freshly ground black pepper
2 teaspoons unsalted butter (or trans-fat free margarine)
1/2 cup shredded Colby Jack cheese
1 cup shredded lettuce
4 tablespoons salsa
2 tablespoons sour cream, optional
2 sprigs fresh cilantro, optional for garnish
SPECIAL EQUIPMENT: 10 inch non-stick pan

directions

1. Put the eggs, water, salt and pepper in a bowl and whisk until frothy.

2. Melt 1 teaspoon of the butter in the pan over medium-high heat, pour in half of the egg mixture and let cook for 1 to 2 minutes. Turn the egg wrap over and let cook for another minute until done.

3. Remove from heat, sprinkle with half the cheese, lettuce, salsa and sour cream and roll up like a burrito. Serve hot garnished with a sprig of fresh cilantro if desired. Repeat the process with the remaining ingredients to make a second wrap.

 # GEORGE'S TIPS:

These Cheese Burrito Omelet Wraps may be wrapped with parchment paper or plastic wrap and kept fresh refrigerated or frozen for a microwave ready anytime meal or snack. Try adding a couple spoonfuls of chili to "beef it up" if desired!

PREP TIME
10 MINS

COOK TIME
10 MINS

SERVES
4

calories 235 | fat 15g | protein 24g | fiber 0g

net carbs 1

DAVID'S BREAKFAST SKILLET
recipe by David Jackson

David or "Wiccanmalenurse" is our resident nurse on our forums at StellaStyle.com, but mostly he is everyone's friend. You can't find a more caring, considerate and knowledgeable individual! David's weight loss success (over 150 pounds down) is well known around our forums and so is this recipe! A creamy and satisfying breakfast, all in one skillet.

shopping list

1/2 pound ground beef or sausage
2 tablespoons onion, finely minced
3 ounces cream cheese
3 large eggs
1 tablespoon water
dash of salt and pepper

directions

1. Brown the ground beef and onions in skillet over medium-high heat and drain excess fat.

2. Turn the heat down to low, add cream cheese and cook just until melted

3. Beat eggs with the water, add the salt and pepper and pour into skillet with beef and cheese. Scramble until done to your liking and serve!

 ## GEORGE'S TIPS:

Try it with ground turkey or turkey sausage to lower the fat!

starters

FIVE SPICE CHINESE CHICKEN SKEWERS
WITH INSTANT PEANUT DIPPING SAUCE

PIZZA STUFFED ZUCCHINI BITES

CHEESY BAKED ARTICHOKE
AND SPINACH DIP

GRILLED ROSEMARY SHRIMP SKEWERS
WITH CUCUMBER RELISH

GRILLED HONEY GLAZED PEACHES AND
CHEESE BROCHETTES

COCONUT / ALMOND SHRIMP WITH
KIWI CHUTNEY

BALTIMORE BAKED CRAB DIP

TERIYAKI SESAME WINGS

ANTIPASTA ON A STICK

BAKED BLACKENED WINGS

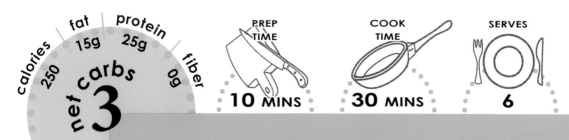

calories 250 | fat 15g | protein 25g | fiber 0g

net carbs **3**

PREP TIME **10** MINS

COOK TIME **30** MINS

SERVES **6**

starters

FIVE SPICE CHINESE CHICKEN SKEWERS WITH INSTANT PEANUT DIPPING SAUCE

If you love Chinese food like me, you will recognize the addictive flavor of these Asian appetizer delights! Chinese Five Spice Powder is a seasoning that is available in stores, but it most likely has sugars added and worse yet it may have MSG! Here, I have duplicated the flavors without all the bad stuff we don't need so indulge five times over for all I care!

directions

1. Preheat the oven to 400 F. Spray a sheet pan with vegetable oil spray and set aside.

2. To make a rub, place all the skewer ingredients, except the chicken, into a medium bowl and mix well.

3. Add the chicken to the bowl and coat each piece with the rub.

4. Place the coated chicken pieces on the greased sheet pan, top with any remaining rub that can be scraped from from the bowl, and bake for approximately 25 – 30 minutes (make certain chicken is cooked thoroughly, juices should run clear when cut into).

5. Remove the cooked chicken thighs from the oven and cool for 10 minutes before cutting lengthwise into 3 strips each.

6. Working over a clean sheet pan, thread 1 cooked chicken strip onto each skewer and leave on the sheet pan.

7. Lightly grill each fully cooked chicken skewer for about 1 minute before serving or simply reheat in the 400 F. oven for 5 minutes. Serve with Peanut Dipping Sauce.

Peanut Dipping Sauce

1. Mix all ingredients together in a small bowl.

shopping list

CHICKEN SKEWERS
vegetable oil spray
3 tablespoons canola oil
1 1/4 teaspoons kosher salt
1/2 teaspoon cinnamon
1/4 teaspoon ground allspice
1/4 teaspoon ground ginger
1/4 teaspoon ground nutmeg
1/4 teaspoon freshly ground black pepper
1/8 teaspoon ground cloves
4 teaspoons sugar substitute (recommended: Splenda)
2 pounds boneless and skinless chicken thighs
18 eight inch bamboo skewers

PEANUT DIPPING SAUCE
1 tablespoon natural peanut butter
2 tablespoons teriyaki sauce
3 teaspoons sugar substitute

 ## GEORGE'S TIPS:

Boneless and skinless chicken breasts may be used for a lower fat alternative to the thigh meat.

calories 85 | fat 5g | protein 5g | fiber 1g

net carbs **3**

PREP TIME **15 MINS**

COOK TIME **4 MINS**

SERVES **8**

starters

PIZZA STUFFED ZUCCHINI BITES

We almost always have fresh zucchini on hand in the Stella household as it is one of the most versatile and affordable veggies. These quick and healthy pizza flavored bites are not only a satisfying cravings buster but an interesting and delicious start to any meal! Go green and eat zucchini! The pizza delivery drivers can save their gas. (And carbs!)

directions

1. Place the oven rack in the second position from the top, preheat the broiler to high and spray the sheet pan with vegetable oil.

2. Layout the zucchini slices flat onto the center of the greased sheet pan and spoon a small amount of sauce over each piece. Then place equal amounts of shredded cheese on each and sprinkle with dry oregano and olive oil.

3. Standing by the oven, broil for about 4 minutes or until cheese is bubbly and brown. Remove and serve hot.

shopping list

vegetable oil spray

2 large zucchini, sliced 1/4 inch thick on a bias into approximately 16 pieces total

1/2 cup **TOMATO AL FRESCO SAUCE**, recipe page: 55

1 cup mozzarella cheese, shredded

1/4 teaspoon dry oregano

1 teaspoon extra virgin olive oil

SPECIAL EQUIPMENT: 1/2 size non-stick sheet pan

GEORGE'S TIPS:

When you first remove the zucchini slices they may appear undercooked but I assure you that within a minute after coming out of the oven the "carry-over cooking" will take care of that and they will be crisp yet tender and most delicious!

Try topping these with your favorite toppings, just like a real pizza. From pepperoni to sausage and mushrooms, why not try them all!

PREP TIME	COOK TIME	SERVES	
10 MINS	**25 MINS**	**6**	

calories **230** / fat **19g** / protein **10g** / fiber **2g**

net carbs 4

starters

CHEESY BAKED ARTICHOKE AND SPINACH DIP

As one of the most popular restaurant starters, I have been making this recipe for decades. The only modification I have made here is that in place of corn starch as a thickener I put in more of the good stuff like three different cheeses!

directions

1. Place the rack in the center position, preheat the oven to 350 degrees F. and spray the casserole dish with vegetable oil.

2. Next add all the ingredients except the mozzarella into a large bowl, mix well and pour into the greased baking dish.

3. Top with the shredded mozzarella and bake for 25 minutes until browned.

shopping list

8 ounces cream cheese, softened
1/2 cup grated Parmesan cheese
1/4 cup sour cream
1 tablespoon chopped red onion
1/2 teaspoon minced fresh garlic
1 teaspoon dry oregano (may use dry or fresh basil)
1/4 teaspoon kosher salt
1/4 teaspoon freshly ground black pepper
1/4 teaspoon garlic powder
1 1/4 cups marinated artichoke hearts, drained well and large chopped
1 cup frozen chopped spinach, thawed and drained well
1/2 cup mozzarella cheese, shredded
SPECIAL EQUIPMENT: 8 inch oven proof glass baking dish or pie pan

4. Remove from the oven and serve hot with a dollop of sour cream on top. Use as a dip for cucumber slices, celery sticks, julienne fresh bell peppers, mushrooms and good carb whole wheat flatbreads or crisps!

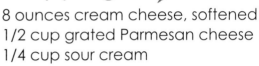

GEORGE'S TIPS:

Low fat or fat free cream cheese, or Neufchatel cheese may be used in place of the cream cheese. Fat free sour cream is another good idea if you are watching fat.

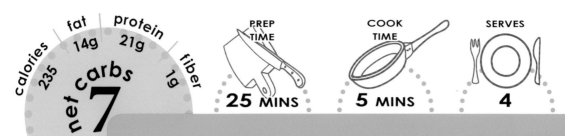

calories 235 · **fat** 14g · **protein** 21g · **fiber** 1g

net carbs 7

PREP TIME 25 MINS · **COOK TIME** 5 MINS · **SERVES** 4

starters

GRILLED ROSEMARY SHRIMP SKEWERS WITH CUCUMBER RELISH

By now you must realize that if I can put in on a stick, I will! There is no better candidate for sticking than deliciously decadent herb coated shrimp refreshed with a cool cucumber relish!

directions

1. Preheat the grill to medium high or use an indoor grill top or grill pan over high heat.
2. Place all the ingredients except the shrimp in a rectangle baking dish large enough for the skewers and mix well.
3. Add the shrimp and toss to coat.
4. Thread 5 pieces of shrimp onto each of the 4 skewers and place back into the dish with the remaining marinade and wait at least 15 minutes before cooking.
5. Place the shrimp skewers on the edges of the grill with the longest part of the stick hanging over the edge away from the fire. Stay close and turn the sticks as needed to prevent burning as skewers are done in just 4 or 5 minutes. Serve hot off the grill with Cucumber Relish over each and garnished with a sprig of whole rosemary if desired.

shopping list

SHRIMP SKEWERS
1/4 cup olive oil (may also use canola oil)
2 tablespoons diced red onion
1 teaspoon fresh chopped garlic
2 tablespoons fresh chopped rosemary leaves
1/2 teaspoon kosher salt
1/4 teaspoon freshly ground black pepper
1 tablespoon fresh lemon juice
1 pound raw large shrimp, peeled and deviened with tail on
4 - 9-inch bamboo skewers

CUCUMBER RELISH
1 cup diced seedless cucumber
2 tablespoons diced dill pickle or relish
1 tablespoon diced red bell pepper
1 tablespoon diced green bell pepper
1 tablespoon fresh lemon juice
1/4 teaspoon kosher salt
1/8 teaspoon freshly ground black pepper

Cucumber Relish

1. Mix the ingredients together well in a glass bowl and chill overnight before serving. If serving immediately, place all ingredients in a food processor and pulse for just a couple of seconds to bring out all the flavors instantly! Be careful not to over chop.

GEORGE'S TIPS:

Have your very own Italian Festival when you pair these shrimp with a comforting *Grilled Chicken Parmesan Casserole*!

calories 177 | fat 8g | protein 6g | fiber 1g | net carbs **20**

PREP TIME 10 MINS

COOK TIME 2 MINS

SERVES 6

starters

GRILLED HONEY GLAZED PEACHES AND CHEESE BROCHETTES

These brochettes are delicious in their simplicity and are great both as an appetizer, or as an after dinner delight! I developed this recipe especially for The Celebration of Connecticut Farms, an event where local Connecticut farmers showcase their artisan handmade and raised goods.

directions

1. Cut the peaches in half and remove the pits by hand. Cut the halves into thirds, making 6 wedges per peach and a total of 18 pieces.

2. Skewer 1 peach wedge onto a bamboo skewer near the end and repeat to make 18 skewers.

3. Lightly grill the peach brochettes for only a minute or less on each side just to make grill marks and lightly heat the peach wedge.

4. Remove from the grill, place on a plate and drizzle with honey and top with crumbled blue cheese or chevre goat cheese-your choice!

shopping list

3 orchard fresh peaches

18 pieces bamboo skewers (may use fresh rosemary sprigs)

4 ounces raw and unprocessed honey

6 ounces blue cheese or chevre cheese (make 9 of each!)

SPECIAL EQUIPMENT: outdoor grill, indoor grill or grill pan. Note: If you do not have a grill, simply pan sear the peach wedges over high heat for just a minute and then place on skewers.

GEORGE'S TIPS:

Press the cheese into the center of the grilled and honey coated peach wedge to make it stay put for serving!

calories 350 | fat 22g | protein 29g | fiber 3g | net carbs **8**

PREP TIME: **10 MINS**

COOK TIME: **4 MINS**

SERVES: **2**

starters

COCONUT / ALMOND SHRIMP WITH KIWI CHUTNEY

Two great recipes in one! We always have shrimp in our freezer for samples at our personal appearances and there always seems to be unsweetened coconut hiding in the freezer. It was only a matter of time before they found each other in such a dramatic fashion, the Kiwi Chutney looking on with admiration.

directions

1. Place a deep, heavy pot over medium-high heat and fill with at least 2 inches of oil. Heat the oil to 350° F. It's very important to monitor and maintain the temperature, or the breading and oil will burn. Portable deep fryers are great, but if you do not have one, you can use a candy thermometer. Just be careful!

2. In a bowl mix the eggs and water to create the egg wash.

3. Put the sliced almonds in a large bowl. Put the shredded coconut in another large bowl.

4. Dip all the shrimp into the egg first and then fully coat 1/4 pound of shrimp in almonds and the other 1/4 pound in coconut.

5. Carefully place the almond breaded shrimp one at a time into the hot oil. Use a slotted spoon and fry until golden brown, about 2 minutes. Try not to stir too much as the breading may fall off before browning, just flip each shrimp once halfway through. After finished, remove from the oil and drain on paper towels. Repeat for coconut breaded shrimp. Serve with Kiwi Chutney.

Kiwi Chutney

1. Mix all the ingredients together.

shopping list

COCONUT / ALMOND SHRIMP
3 to 6 cups canola oil (depending on size of pot used)
2 eggs
1 tablespoon water
1 cup sliced almonds
1 cup unsweetened shredded coconut
1/2 pound large shrimp, peeled and deveined (filet open and flat)
1/4 teaspoon salt
1/8 fresh ground black pepper
KIWI CHUTNEY
2 kiwi fruits, peeled and diced
1 tablespoon diced yellow bell pepper (or any color)
1 tablespoon diced gold bell pepper (or any color)
1 tablespoon diced red onion
1 teaspoon fresh lemon juice
1 teaspoon sugar substitute (recommended: Splenda)

GEORGE'S TIPS:

To help reduce fat you may bake the shrimp on a vegetable sprayed sheet pan at 400° F. for about 15 minutes or until golden brown.

PREP TIME
15 MINS

COOK TIME
25 MINS

SERVES
8

calories 265 | fat 24g | protein 14g | fiber 0g

net carbs
2

starters

BALTIMORE BAKED CRAB DIP

I have always been a big fan of blue crabs which are not only prevalent in Maryland but my older sister Steph used to catch her share of them in south Florida and I almost always left with a bucket full when I visited her. This is yet another way to use them that calls for the less expensive claw meat which, in my opinion, has all the flavor! Once you add in the Old Bay seasoning, you might as well be in Baltimore!

directions

1. Place the rack in the center position, preheat the oven to 350 degrees F. and spray the casserole dish with vegetable oil.

shopping list 🖉

vegetable oil spray
8 ounces cream cheese, softened
8 ounces blue crab claw meat (may use lump)
2 cups cheddar cheese, shredded
1/2 cup sour cream
2 tablespoons green onion tops and a few more for garnish, thinly sliced
1 tablespoon roasted red peppers, diced
1 teaspoon Old Bay seasoning and 1/4 teaspoon more
1/8 teaspoon garlic powder
1/4 teaspoon freshly ground black pepper
SPECIAL EQUIPMENT: 8 inch oven proof glass baking dish or pie pan

2. Next add all the ingredients into a large bowl mix well and pour into the greased baking dish and sprinkle with 1/4 teaspoon Old Bay seasoning.

3. Bake for 25 minutes until bubbly and starting to brown.

4. Remove from the oven, throw a few thin slices of green onions on top and serve hot as a dip for cucumber slices, celery sticks, julienne fresh bell peppers, mushrooms and good carb whole wheat flatbreads or crisps!

 GEORGE'S TIPS:

Low fat or fat free cream cheese, or Neufchatel cheese may be used in place of the cream cheese. Low fat cheddar cheese is another good idea if you are watching fat.

calories 570
fat 27g
protein 68g
fiber 0g
net carbs **6**

PREP TIME **2-3** HRS

COOK TIME **60** MINS

SERVES **8**

starters

TERIYAKI SESAME WINGS

Okay, say you were having a chicken wing party. You are? That's crazy, so am I! You should make these Teriyaki Sesame Wings and watch as football players literally climb through your television to grab a few. Who knows, you could change the course of sports history here. (Or at least eat some really great wings!)

directions

1. Add all the ingredients, except the wings to a large bowl and mix well. Add the wings and toss to coat. Cover and refrigerate for at least 2 hours, tossing them in the bowl a couple times during the marinating process.

shopping list

vegetable oil spray

15 ounces teriyaki sauce (recommended: Kikkoman with 2 grams sugar per serving)

6 tablespoons sesame oil

1 tablespoon fresh ginger root, peeled and minced

1 teaspoon minced fresh garlic

2 tablespoons fresh lemon juice (1 lemon)

2 tablespoons sugar substitute (recommended: Splenda)

4 pounds fresh chicken wings, wing tips cut off

SPECIAL EQUIPMENT: 1/2 size sheet pan or baking dish

2. Preheat the oven to 375 degrees F. and spray the sheet pan with vegetable oil.

3. Pull the wings from the marinade, place on the sheet pan and bake for 1 hour until skin becomes crispy. If not crispy, simply turn the broiler on high and let them crisp up for only a couple minutes while you stand there watching them. Remove and serve!

GEORGE'S TIPS:

For wings with a little citrus "tang" replace the lemon juice and sugar substitute with a dry tablespoon of "Sunrise Orange Crystal Light" or "Sugar-Free Tang" dry drink mix.

Baking these wings instead of deep fat frying has already lightened up the fats considerably. You can also opt for delicious teriyaki sesame, boneless, skinless chicken breasts prepared the same way, but only baked for about 30 – 35 minutes until done.

calories 500 | fat 40g | protein 27g | fiber 2g | **net carbs 6**

PREP TIME 35 MINS | **COOK TIME** 0 MINS | **SERVES** 8

starters

ANTIPASTA ON A STICK

I know, I'm on a stick-kick but who doesn't like kebobs? Get your kids in the kitchen to help make these fun starters that are simple to make, present and eat. Simple goes a long way when you are entertaining and with make-ahead items like this you always get more time with your guests!

directions

1. Add all the ingredients up to the mushrooms into a bowl and whisk together. Then add the mushrooms and artichokes and refrigerate for 30 minutes while preparing the remaining ingredients.

2. Wrap each pepperoncini with a small piece of prosciutto and thread the 16 skewers from bottom to top with a piece of wrapped pepperoncini, roasted pepper, black olive, mushroom, mozzarella cheese, salami, artichoke, tomato and black olive. Serve cold drizzled with any remaining marinade from the mushrooms and garnished with fresh basil leaves if desired.

shopping list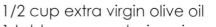

1/2 cup extra virgin olive oil
1 tablespoon red wine vinegar
1 tablespoon fresh lemon juice
1 teaspoon fresh basil leaves, chopped
1/4 teaspoon fresh garlic, minced
1/4 teaspoon kosher salt
1/8 teaspoon freshly ground black pepper
12 ounces small button mushrooms, whole or cut into 16 equal pieces
8 ounces marinated artichoke hearts, quartered into 16 pieces
16 pieces small pepperoncini, mild or hot
1/2 pound prosciutto, thinly sliced and cut into 16 equal lengths
8 ounces fresh mozzarella cheese, cut into 16 equal chunks
8 ounces roasted red pepper strips, cut into 16 pieces
32 pieces cured black pitted olives, may use kalamata or ripe
16 pieces small cherry tomatoes
1 pound Genoa salami, cut 1 inch thick at the deli and then into 16 – 1 inch squares
SPECIAL EQUIPMENT: 16 medium length bamboo skewers

GEORGE'S TIPS:

Use any deli meats you like; others we use are mortadella, capicolla and soppresata dried Italian sausage! When you get bored – go Greek by replacing the basil with oregano in the marinade and use Feta cheese and Greek olives in place of the Italian ingredients!

PREP TIME
10 MINS

COOK TIME
60 MINS

SERVES
8

calories 470 — fat 20g — protein 65g — fiber 0g
net carbs 0

BAKED BLACKENED WINGS

Besides trying to cook and eat healthier we are always looking to simplify things in the Stella kitchen. With this recipe my days (and yours) of heating up a ton of hot oil to cook wings are over. Why bother if they can be as tasty and crispy without all the fuss and muss and fat of deep fried? Because we always have our all purpose Blackening Spice on hand it makes it super fast to get this dinner in the oven and relax while it cooks!

shopping list

vegetable oil spray
4 pounds fresh chicken wings
2 tablespoons extra virgin olive oil (may use canola oil)
2 tablespoons plus 1 tablespoon more Blackening Spice; recipe page 57
SPECIAL EQUIPMENT: 1/2 size sheet pan or baking dish

directions

1. Preheat the oven to 375 degrees F. and spray the sheet pan with vegetable oil.

2. Add the wings, oil and 2 tablespoons of Blackening Spice to a large bowl and toss to coat well.

3. Place the coated wings on the sheet pan and sprinkle them evenly with the remaining 1 tablespoon of Blackening Spice and bake for 1 hour until skin becomes crispy. Remove and serve as is or toss them in a 50-50 mixture of Louisiana hot sauce and melted butter for spicy Buffalo wings!

 ## GEORGE'S TIPS:

Baking these wings instead of deep fat frying has already lightened up the fats considerably. You can also opt for blackened, boneless skinless chicken breasts prepared the same way, but only baked for about 30 – 35 minutes until done.

Ten Tips for Cooking with Kids

Recently, I've spent a lot of time with organizations like the Junior Leagues in an effort to get more kids in the kitchen, cooking with their parents. Not only is it an activity that can bring the whole family together but it encourages creativity and independence from high calorie restaurant food. Even the most finicky kids will be more apt to try something (like a new vegetable) if they had a hand in making it. Here, I've compiled a few tips for cooking with your kids.

1. Teach the essentials.
Hand washing, clean surfaces and safety are of the utmost importance. You're having fun, but keep the fun away from anything hot or sharp!

2. Let them make a mess!
Cooking should be enjoyable, especially if you ever want them to do it again. Getting a little dirty is always fun.

3. Dress as a chef.
A child's size apron and even a chef's hat, if you can find it, will not only make your kid feel like the real thing but the apron will catch some of that mess you're letting them make.

4. Plan for safety.
Obviously you don't want to hand your six year old a ten inch chef's knife, so try to plan meals that require less chopping, as they'll get the most pride from making something themselves from start to finish. Instead of chopping zucchinis, try snapping fresh green beans by hand for example.

5. Use plastic instead of glass.
It's always a good idea to have plastic mixing bowls, measuring cups and other non-breakable kitchen essentials around when kids are involved.

6. Follow along to a recipe in this book!
Go for a recipe with a picture and see how close you can make it to the picture.

7. Write your own recipe!
Buy ingredients that you know will work together in a casserole or similar dish, then let your child come up with just the right way to put it together, writing it down all along the way. Of course they should name it as well! There are even blank recipe pages at the end of this book!

8. Be their helper.
You should be your child's helper, not the other way around! They'll never want to cook with you again if all they get to do is watch!

9. Clean up!
Cleaning up after yourself as you go is integral for any chef and can't be taught too soon. Hopefully it's a value that can extend itself outside of the kitchen too!

10. Eat as a family!
Even if you don't have the time to cook together, this one is a no brainer.

condiments, sauces and staples

ALMOND FLOUR

MINT BUTTER

TOMATO AL FRESCO SAUCE

BLACKENING SPICE

FRESH RASPBERRY FRUIT DIP

LEMON POPPY GINGER DRESSING

CRANBERRY WALNUT CHUTNEY

QUICK AND EASY KETCHUP

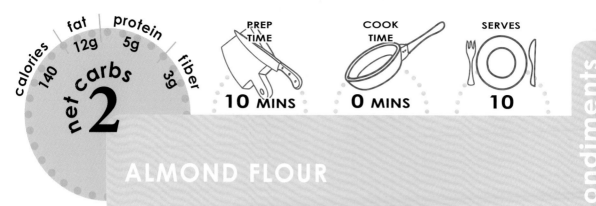

calories 140 | fat 12g | protein 5g | fiber 3g | net carbs 2

PREP TIME **10 MINS** | COOK TIME **0 MINS** | SERVES **10**

ALMOND FLOUR

Using ground almonds as an alternative to white flour is just plain good all the way around! Almonds are loaded with fiber and are a strong antioxidant with heart-healthy monounsaturated fats that take the place of saturated or trans-fats in recipes.

shopping list

10 ounces whole raw almonds (we buy a 10oz bag found in the produce department or baking isle)

May use sliced almonds.

directions

1. Grind almonds on high in a food processor for about 3 minutes until a grainy flour consistency.

makes 2 1/2 cups almond flour

 GEORGE'S TIPS:

Almond flour can be stored in an airtight container up to 1 week on the counter or several months in the freezer.

Some recipes in this book call for almond flour made from blanched almonds, which gives the flour an even, white flour look. Blanched almonds are most often found cut in slivers in the baking aisle.

PREP TIME
5 MINS

COOK TIME
0 MINS

SERVES
4

calories 40
fat 4.5g
protein 0g
fiber 0g
net carbs 0

MINT BUTTER

Classic cooking is simple and it doesn't get any easier than this! I am a big advocate of fresh herbs in cooking and why not as they add flavor and flair instantly to almost any meal. Don't stop at mint; try basil, cilantro or dill and open up a whole world of possibilities!

shopping list

2 tablespoons trans-fat free margarine (or real butter)

2 tablespoons chopped fresh mint leaves

1/8 teaspoon kosher salt

directions

1. In a bowl use a fork to mix together all the ingredients until well blended. Keep refrigerated in a sealed container for up to 1 week or freeze for much longer.

 ## GEORGE'S TIPS:

Try this recipe to top off the finished *Fearless Roast Rack of Lamb,* recipe page: 133, before serving but it's also great on chicken, pork or added to vegetables for instant gourmet flavor!

calories 74
fat 7g
protein 5g
net carbs 2.5
fiber 1g

PREP TIME 10 MINS
COOK TIME 5 MINS
SERVES 4

TOMATO AL FRESCO SAUCE

There is no need to spend all day cooking a tomato sauce and there is certainly no need to use a bland store bought sauce loaded with added sugars! This simple, quick sauce is Italian in a pinch. A pinch of this and a pinch of that and you're eating good!

shopping list

2 tablespoons extra virgin olive oil
2 tablespoons diced red onion
2 teaspoons fresh chopped garlic
2 tablespoons fresh chopped basil leaves
1/2 teaspoon kosher salt
1/4 teaspoon freshly ground black pepper
1 1/2 cups diced plum or vine ripe tomatoes

directions

1. Heat the oil in a saucepan over medium heat. Add all the ingredients and cook, stirring for about 5 minutes. Remove and serve hot or cool and store refrigerated for 3 days or frozen for up to 6 months.

GEORGE'S TIPS:

Skip the stove and mix all of the ingredients cold, then refrigerate for a few hours to bring out the flavors and make a simple bruschetta you can serve over crispy whole wheat flatbread.

calories 5 | fat 0g | protein 0g | fiber 0g

net carbs 0

PREP TIME
10 MINS

COOK TIME
0 MINS

SERVES
MANY

condiments

BLACKENING SPICE

This has got to be one of the most versatile and valuable spices in our kitchen. You can instantly use this seasoning mix to not only blacken everything from chicken and fish to pork chops and steaks, but we even season our vegetables with it! Most importantly, it makes a great alternative to store bought steak seasonings that are full of sugar, MSG and fillers—eek!

shopping list

5 tablespoons kosher salt
5 tablespoons paprika
1 tablespoon dry thyme
1 tablespoon ground black pepper
1 tablespoon garlic powder
1/2 teaspoon cayenne pepper
1/2 teaspoon ground white pepper

directions

1. Mix all the blackening spice ingredients well and store in a sealed container or spice canister.

makes 1 shaker full

GEORGE'S TIPS:

You will never regret having a spice jar of this stuff around! It's an everyday dinner idea in a pinch.

condiments

PREP TIME
10 MINS

COOK TIME
0 MINS

SERVES
16

calories 60
fat 5g
protein 1g
fiber 1g
net carbs 1

FRESH RASPBERRY FRUIT DIP

Dip into this great treat! Sliced apples, cantaloupe, honeydew and a batch of this fresh raspberry fruit dip and you're ready for a party. Well you'll probably need some music at your party too, but I don't have a recipe for that... yet. However, this recipe comes close to creating music in your mouth. Just don't double dip!

directions

1. Keep a few raspberries aside and place all the remaining ingredients into the food processor or blender and pulse until somewhat smooth.

2. Remove, pour in a glass bowl or cantaloupe half and top with the few whole raspberries and sprigs of fresh mint for garnish. Serve as a dip right away or store in a non-reactive covered container and keep refrigerated for up to 3 days.

shopping list
8 ounces cream cheese

1 full pint fresh raspberries, (they usually come in 1/2 pint containers, you will need 2)

1 teaspoon fresh lime juice

1 teaspoon fresh lemon juice (may use all lemon juice if lime is not available)

2 tablespoons sugar substitute (recommended: Splenda)

2 sprigs of fresh mint, optional for garnish

SPECIAL EQUIPMENT: blender or food processor

 ## GEORGE'S TIPS:

Lighten up this cheese spread by choosing low fat or fat free cream cheese in place of regular. If the berries are good and sweet, the sugar substitute may be reduced or left out entirely with sweetness coming naturally from the berries and cream cheese.

calories 40 · fat 2g · protein 2g · fiber 0g · **net carbs 1**

PREP TIME **10 MINS**

COOK TIME **0 MINS**

SERVES **4**

condiments

LEMON POPPY GINGER DRESSING

Rachel loves this Asian flare dressing and therefore I have no doubt you will too; if you know what's good for you! From the zing of the lemon to the zest of the fresh ginger, your taste buds will be satisfied. Make any salad great with this delightful creamy vinaigrette.

directions

1. In a blender or food processor on high speed, combine the mustard, lemon juice, vinegar, ginger, sugar substitute and garlic powder for a few seconds until smooth. Turn the blender down to medium speed and slowly add the oil in a continuous stream.

shopping list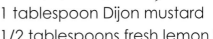

1 tablespoon Dijon mustard
1/2 tablespoons fresh lemon juice
2 tablespoons red wine vinegar
1 tablespoon fresh ginger root, peeled and minced
1 packet sugar substitute (recommended: Splenda packet, or 2 teaspoons granulated)
1/2 teaspoon garlic powder
1/2 cup canola oil
1/2 teaspoon salt
1/8 teaspoon freshly ground black pepper
1/2 teaspoon poppy seeds
SPECIAL EQUIPMENT: blender or mini food processor

2. Season with salt and pepper and stir in the poppy seeds to finish. Pour into a non reactive glass or plastic container and keep refrigerated for up to 2 weeks.

 # GEORGE'S TIPS:

Extra virgin olive oil may be used in place of the canola as another heart healthy alternative. You may even leave the oil out all together and replace it with water for an entirely fat free alternative to normal salad dressing.

calories 52 | fat 3g | protein 1g | fiber 2g

net carbs 4

PREP TIME **5 MINS**

COOK TIME **15 MINS**

SERVES **12**

condiments

CRANBERRY WALNUT CHUTNEY

Turkey is a big favorite 'round the Stella household and nothing goes better with turkey than cranberry sauce! Well, we always have cranberries in the freezer and I had a lone golden delicious apple in the fridge, then turkey breast went on sale and the perfect storm was at hand! Simple and delicious, this recipe is sure to become a staple at your family table as it is at ours.

shopping list

1 cup sugar substitute (recommended: Splenda)

1 cup water

12 ounces fresh or frozen cranberries

1 golden delicious apple, cored and small diced (may use any apple)

1 teaspoon freshly grated orange zest

1/2 teaspoon vanilla extract

1/4 teaspoon cinnamon

1/2 cup chopped walnuts

directions

1. Combine the sugar substitute and water in a saucepan and bring to a boil over high heat.

2. Add the remaining ingredients, bring back to a boil. Reduce the heat to low and simmer for 10 minutes, stirring occasionally.

3. Remove from the heat, cool and refrigerate for at least one hour before serving cold.

GEORGE'S TIPS:

Before cooking, rinse and pick through the raw cranberries to remove rotten berries and stems.

condiments

PREP TIME
5 MINS

COOK TIME
0 MINS

SERVES
24

calories 10 · fat 0g · protein 1g · fiber 0g
net carbs 2

QUICK AND EASY KETCHUP

A quick and easy way to make our own ketchup alternative was one of the first things we had to invent! Nothing fancy, but it sure does the trick without all those corn syrup solids you get with store bought.

shopping list

8 ounces tomato sauce, no sugar added

6 ounces tomato paste, no sugar added

2 tablespoons white vinegar

1/4 cup sugar substitute (recommended: Splenda)

directions

1. Mix all ingredients together in a small bowl. Keep refrigerated for up to 1 week.

 GEORGE'S TIPS:

Mix with mayonnaise for a quick and easy, no sugar added Russian dressing.

salads, soups and slow cookers

WILTED SPINACH SALAD WITH
WALNUTS AND APPLES

HOT AND SOUR SOUP

SOUTHWESTERN CHICKEN TACO STEW

ALMOND CRUSTED CHICKEN SALAD
WITH SWEET MUSTARD SAUCE

BROCCOLI AND CHEESE SOUP

SEVEN LAYER SALAD

CREAMY LIME GELATIN DELIGHT

SLOW COOKER BBQ PULLED PORK

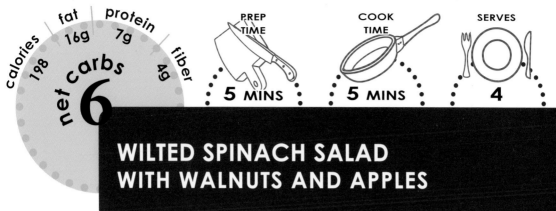

salads/soups

calories 198 | fat 16g | protein 7g | fiber 4g

net carbs **6**

PREP TIME **5 MINS** | COOK TIME **5 MINS** | SERVES **4**

WILTED SPINACH SALAD WITH WALNUTS AND APPLES

Spinach salads are classic and this one is simple, healthy and the presentation is as good as any 5 star restaurant! Get everybody to say, "Whoa, did you make that?"

directions

1. Add the oil, walnuts and apples to a large sauté pan and cook for 4 minutes over medium high heat.

2. Next add the raw spinach, salt and pepper to the hot pan and remove from the heat. Using tongs or a large kitchen spoon, toss until well coated with the mixture.

3. Working quickly, place the ring mold in the center of a large dinner plate, fill with the spinach mixture and pat down to compress and help keep it's shape. While holding the spinach mixture down with a few fingers of one hand use the other hand to carefully lift the ring mold straight up and off the plate, leaving the compressed spinach salad behind.

4. Repeat for all 4 salads sprinkling the plates evenly with any leftover walnuts, apples and oil from the pan. Garnish each plate with diced red bell pepper if desired.

shopping list

2 tablespoons extra virgin olive oil
1/2 cup shelled walnut halves
1 cup thin sliced granny smith apples (about 1 apple)
1 tablespoon lemon juice, squeezed over the apple once sliced
1/2 teaspoon kosher salt
1/4 teaspoon fresh ground black pepper
1 pound cleaned fresh baby spinach leaves
1 tablespoon diced red bell pepper, optional for garnish
SPECIAL EQUIPMENT: ring mold, can be made from a 1 liter plastic bottle by using a serrated knife to cut a 4 inch wide ring from the center

 GEORGE'S TIPS:

Kick off a great grilling day with this refreshing salad!

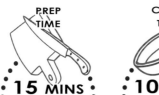
PREP TIME
15 MINS

COOK TIME
10 MINS

SERVES
8

calories **201**
fat **12g**
protein **18g**
fiber **2g**
net carbs **3**

HOT AND SOUR SOUP

Who doesn't love Chinese food? While Wonton Soup may get all the attention, I've always been a huge fan of the tangy and wonderful Hot and Sour Soup. My take on it took a whole lotta experimenting, but I think I've cracked the code. It's hot. It's sour. It's inexplicably good.

directions

1. Place a wok or large sauté pan over high heat with the canola oil until almost smoking hot. Add the pork strips, ginger and garlic and stir for just a minute until pork is cooked.

2. Add the remaining ingredients except the sesame oil and eggs and cook for about 5 minutes more.

3. Remove from heat and slowly pour in the beaten eggs and let sit for two minutes until cooked from the heat of the soup.

shopping list

2 tablespoons canola oil

8 ounces boneless pork loin, cut into small strips (may use any pork or chicken)

1 tablespoon fresh grated ginger

1/2 teaspoon fresh garlic, minced

4 cups chicken broth

1/4 cup soy sauce

1 1/2 tablespoons cider vinegar (white vinegar will work too)

8 ounces straw mushrooms, drained

4 ounces bamboo shoots, drained

2 cups firm tofu, cut into 1 inch squares (usually sold in 15.5 ounce packages)

1/8 teaspoon crushed red pepper flakes, optional for added "heat"

2 tablespoons sesame oil

2 eggs, beaten

2 tablespoons green onion tops, chopped (for garnish)

SPECIAL EQUIPMENT: wok or large saute pan

4. To finish, gently stir in the sesame oil and serve hot topped with chopped green onions.

 ## GEORGE'S TIPS:

Bake a few whole wheat pitas at 350 degrees and break into the soup like fried wontons!

calories 320
fat 18g
protein 32g
fiber 4g
net carbs 5

PREP TIME **15** MINS

COOK TIME **4-8** HRS

SERVES **12**

salads/soups

SOUTHWESTERN CHICKEN TACO STEW

Set it and forget it with this Mexican slow cooker stew that your whole family will love! I say, let dinner cook itself, you've got more important things to do. Whether you can concentrate on other things with the great aromas throughout the house is something else entirely!

directions

1. Add all the ingredients, except the chicken and garnish, into a slow cooker and mix.

2. Place the chicken breasts on top and push down into the stew. Cover and cook on high for about 3 1/2-4 hours or on low for 7-8 hours until chicken is falling apart.

3. To finish, remove cooked chicken, shred with a fork and stir back into the stew. Serve topped with shredded cheddar cheese and if desired add a dollop of sour cream and a sprig of fresh cilantro for garnish.

shopping list

1/2 cup Spanish onion, chopped (may use any yellow or white onion)
1 green bell pepper, seeded and large chopped
1 red bell pepper, seeded and large chopped
1 teaspoon fresh minced garlic
1- 15 ounce can black soy beans, drained and rinsed
2- 14.5 ounce cans diced tomatoes w/chilies
1- 8 ounce can tomato sauce
3 tablespoons chili powder
2 tablespoons ground cumin
1/2 teaspoon garlic powder
2 pounds boneless skinless chicken breasts
8 ounces shredded cheddar cheese
1 cup sour cream, optional for garnish
fresh cilantro sprigs, optional for garnish
SPECIAL EQUIPMENT: slow cooker or crock pot

GEORGE'S TIPS:

Crisp up some whole wheat tortillas or pitas in a 350 degree oven for a few minutes and serve alongside this stew for dipping.

calories 550 | fat 30g | protein 46g | fiber 8g | net carbs 14

PREP TIME 10 MINS | COOK TIME 20 MINS | SERVES 4

salads/soups

ALMOND CRUSTED CHICKEN SALAD WITH SWEET MUSTARD SAUCE

Fried chicken salads are a big thing at fast food restaurants nowadays and they couldn't be anything further from healthy! Here, I've taken the frying out of the fried chicken by baking the tenders and taken out the carbs of the breading and sugary dressing to boot.

directions

1. Preheat oven to 400 degrees. Spray sheet pan with vegetable oil cooking spray.

2. Add almond flour, salt, pepper, and paprika to a bowl and mix.

3. Add chicken strips to the seasoned almond flour and toss until well coated.

4. Lay the breaded chicken strips on the greased sheet pan, leaving a space in between.

5. Bake for approximately 20 minutes; until browned and at least 165 degrees when tested with a meat thermometer. (Cut into thickest piece to check if you're not sure.)

6. Assemble the salad ingredients into 4 separate dishes. Lay 3 finished strips over each salad and top with two tablespoons of Sweet Mustard Sauce on each.

shopping list

ALMOND CRUSTED CHICKEN
vegetable oil spray
1/2 cup almond flour
1/2 teaspoon kosher salt
1/4 teaspoon ground black pepper
1/2 teaspoon paprika
1 pound boneless skinless chicken breasts (cut into 12 equal strips)
SALAD
4 hard boiled eggs
4 cups salad mix
8 radicchio leaves
8 leaf lettuce leaves
12 grape tomatoes
4 radishes
SWEET MUSTARD SAUCE
1/2 cup mayonnaise (may use light)
1/4 cup yellow table mustard
2 tablespoons sugar substitute (recommended: Splenda)

Sweet Mustard Sauce

1. Mix all ingredients well in a small bowl.

GEORGE'S TIPS:

This recipe is actually three in one, so feel free to make just the almond crusted chicken tenders and sauce for your next party!

calories 237 | fat 18g | protein 10g | fiber 1g

net carbs 6

PREP TIME **10 MINS**

COOK TIME **15 MINS**

SERVES **4**

BROCCOLI AND CHEESE SOUP

This family classic is a no frills comfort food that we don't have to feel guilty about eating! Without any added starches for thickening, there's no guilt at all!

directions

1. Heat the trans-fat free margarine in a large sauce pan over medium-high heat. Add the red onion, garlic, broccoli, salt, and pepper and cook for about 3 minutes until broccoli is tender.

2. Add the chicken broth and continue to cook for about 4 minutes more until the liquid reduces down by at least a third.

shopping list 🖉

1 tablespoon trans-fat free margarine (may use butter)
1 tablespoon red onion, minced
1/2 teaspoon fresh garlic, minced (1 small clove)
2 cups fresh broccoli crowns, chopped
1/2 teaspoon kosher salt
1/4 teaspoon ground black pepper
2 1/2 cups chicken broth, low sodium
1/2 cup heavy cream (may use half and half or unsweetened soy milk, recommended: Silk brand)
8 slices "Deluxe" American cheese
SPECIAL EQUIPMENT: large sauce pan or small stock pot, blender

3. Remove from the heat; pour half the soup into a blender and puree.

4. Return the puree to the pan, place back over medium-high heat and add the cream.

5. Let cook for just a minute to heat back up and then add the cheese slices one at a time; waiting another minute just until melted. Whisk until the cheese is thoroughly blended into the soup, remove from heat and serve.

 # GEORGE'S TIPS:

Make certain to use "Deluxe" or "Real" American cheese and not "cheese food" for proper melting. Although you can use cheddar, it tends to have too much butter fat and can make this creamy soup "break" or separate.

calories 350 | fat 25g | protein 19g | fiber 1g | net carbs 8

PREP TIME: 30 MINS
COOK TIME: 0 MINS
SERVES: 16

SEVEN LAYER SALAD
recipe by Mary Beth Guard

Mary Beth and Michael Guard are my new best friends in Oklahoma City, Oklahoma! Recently they invited me for a weekend at their home where together with her friends we shopped, cooked and ate all types of wonderful low carb dishes. Mary Beth, being quite the gourmand, made and presented us this wonderfully delicious and very impressive seven layer salad that she has so graciously agreed to share. Thanks Mary Beth! And thanks to Michael for the best coffee I've ever had!

directions

1. Add the dressing ingredients to a bowl and mix well.

2. Toss the cabbage with the dressing and place in the bottom of the bowl as the first layer followed in order by the cheese, peppers, cauliflower, onion, bacon and chicken. Serve from the bottom up so the dressing from the cabbage reaches the other ingredients.

shopping list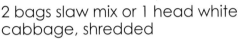

2 bags slaw mix or 1 head white cabbage, shredded
1 1/2 cups shredded cheddar cheese (may use 3/4 cup crumbled bleu cheese)
1 green or red bell pepper, seeded and diced
3/4 head cauliflower, chopped or thinly sliced
1/2 red onion, finely chopped
1 pound bacon, freshly cooked until crispy and large crumbled
2 cups cooked boneless chicken breast, shredded or cubed

DRESSING
2 cups mayonnaise (may use light)
1 tablespoon red wine vinegar
1 tablespoon sugar substitute (recommended: Splenda)
1 teaspoon Beau Monde seasoning

SPECIAL EQUIPMENT: large, clear glass "Truffle" or salad bowl

 ## GEORGE'S TIPS:

You may leave the chicken out if using this salad as a side dish and this salad can be made the day before as it keeps well for several days refrigerated. A cheese grater works perfectly to chop the cauliflower into tiny pieces!

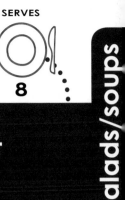

calories 160
fat 10g
protein 11g
fiber 1g
net carbs 3

PREP TIME **10 MINS**
CHILL TIME **4+ HRS**
SERVES **8**

salads/soups

CREAMY LIME GELATIN DELIGHT
recipe by Deloris Finley

Recently I had the pleasure to visit Oklahoma City, where I made many new friends, including Deloris Finley! She knew exactly how to make me a friend for life; she cooked and fed me! This jello salad was only one of the delicious dishes and I must say that Deloris instantly brought comforting memories of my Mom's style of cooking when jello was traditionally combined with all kinds of veggies and put in those cool molds you now hang on your walls for decoration! Thanks a million Deloris!

shopping list

1 large box sugar-free lime gelatin (.6 ounce box that makes eight 1/2 cup servings)
2 cups boiling water
1 cup sugar-free diet lemon-lime soda (may use water)
2 cups small curd cottage cheese
3/4 cup finely chopped pecans
1/2 cup cheddar cheese, finely shredded
2 ribs celery, cleaned and very finely chopped (to resemble crushed pineapple)
SPECIAL EQUIPMENT: 8 x 8 inch jello mold or baking dish sprayed with vegetable oil

directions

1. Add gelatin and boiling water to a large bowl and stir for two minutes until completely dissolved. While stirring add the remaining ingredients one at a time, in the order of the ingredients list.

2. Pour the mixture into the prepared dish and refrigerate for 4 hours or until set. Slice into squares to serve cold.

GEORGE'S TIPS:

This recipe keeps well for several days refrigerated. A food processor works well for chopping the pecans and celery.

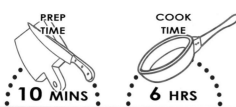

PREP TIME
10 MINS

COOK TIME
6 HRS

SERVES
12

calories **345**
fat **15g**
protein **44g**
fiber **2g**
net carbs **5**

SLOW COOKER BBQ PULLED PORK

Pulled pork is a favorite here in the south. Making it with my special, no sugar added, no-cook BBQ sauce is a favorite of mine! If it wasn't good, I'd have to find a new home, so you know there was a lot on the line with this one!

directions

1. Season the roast liberally with salt and pepper on all sides and place into the slow cooker.

2. Put all the BBQ sauce ingredients into a bowl and whisk well to combine. Pour half the BBQ sauce over the roast and add the water. Cover and cook on high for about 6 hours until pork is falling apart.

3. To finish, remove the roast and shred with two forks. Mix the remainder of the BBQ sauce into the pulled pork to serve or leave the sauce on the side if preferred.

shopping list

4 pounds Boston Butt pork roast (may use any fatty boneless pork)
Salt and ground black pepper
2 cups water

NO-COOK BBQ SAUCE
One 29-ounce can tomato sauce
One 6-ounce can tomato paste
2 tablespoons white vinegar
2 tablespoons liquid smoke
1 tablespoon Worcestershire sauce
1 1/2 teaspoons hot sauce (recommended: Tabasco)
3/4 cup sugar substitute (recommended: Splenda)
2 tablespoons finely chopped red onion
1 small clove garlic, minced
1/4 teaspoon garlic powder
1 tablespoon kosher salt
1 teaspoon ground black pepper
1 teaspoon onion powder
SPECIAL EQUIPMENT: slow cooker or crock pot

 # GEORGE'S TIPS:

This is also a great way to make spareribs, short ribs and even BBQ pulled beef or chicken!

vegetables and sides

TOMATO FROMAGE

NO CORN CORNBREAD

SIMPLY GRILLED VEGETABLES

SCAMPI SAUTEED MUSHROOMS

ASPARAGUS, RED PEPPERS AND PINE NUTS

MOCK MASHED POTATOES SUPREME

BROCCOLI POLONAISE

SPINACH RICOTTA DUMPLINGS

SAVORY GARLIC HERB MUFFINS

TWICE BAKED CANDIED SWEET POTATOES

THE HAYDENS' "HASH BROWN" CASSEROLE

calories 70 | fat 4g | protein 6g | fiber 1g | net carbs 2

PREP TIME **4 MINS**

COOK TIME **12 MINS**

SERVES **3**

veggies / sides

TOMATO FROMAGE

Tomato Fromage is not only an easy-to-make side dish but also a great garnish that appears frequently in French cuisine. I first used it back in the 70's doing Continental cuisine when you would put a Tomato Fromage next to every steak served.

shopping list

vegetable oil spray

3 small or Roma tomatoes

Kosher salt

freshly ground black pepper

garlic powder

1/2 cup grated Parmesan cheese (more or less as desired)

directions

1. Preheat the oven to 350° F. Spray a small baking sheet with vegetable oil spray.

2. Slice a small piece off the top and bottom of each tomato and stand them up on the baking sheet.

3. Sprinkle the tomatoes liberally with salt, pepper, and garlic powder.

4. Carefully pile the Parmesan cheese high on the tops of each tomato.

5. Bake for about 12 minutes, until the cheese starts to turn golden brown.

6. Remove and serve while still warm.

 ## GEORGE'S TIPS:

You can also try this with yellow squash and zucchini sliced in half, length-wise.

calories 120 | fat 7g | protein 9g | fiber 2g | net carbs 5

PREP TIME **10 MINS**

COOK TIME **30 MINS**

SERVES **6**

veggies / sides

NO CORN CORNBREAD

When Rachel said she was going to make cornbread for the first time in six years, I said, "Impossible!" Today, It is evident in the end result that my wife is using some kind of sorcery, or something I will call "corn magic" to bring this bread to the table.

directions

1. Preheat the oven to 375 degrees F.

2. Spray the skillet with the cooking spray. In a small bowl, mix together the bran and 1/2 tablespoon soy flour. Evenly sprinkle the pan with the mixture, being careful to coat the sides.

3. In a larger bowl whisk together the 1 cup soy flour, sugar substitute and baking powder. Add the eggs, heavy cream, vanilla and club soda and continue to whisk until completely blended.

4. Fold in the diced yellow squash, pour the batter into the prepared skillet and bake for about 25 minutes until the top starts to brown. The bread is done when lightly browned and when a toothpick inserted in the center comes out clean.

5. Remove the skillet from the oven and let cool for at least 5 minutes. Carefully loosen the bread around the edges with a spatula, place a large plate over the top of the pan and flip upside down to remove. Cut into 6 pieces to serve warm or cold.

shopping list

vegetable oil spray
1 tablespoon milled flax seed
1 cup plus 1/2 tablespoon soy flour
1/2 cup sugar substitute (recommended: Splenda)
1 1/2 teaspoons baking powder
2 large eggs
1/2 cup heavy cream (may use unsweetened soy milk)
1/3 cup club soda
1 teaspoon vanilla extract
1/3 cup small diced yellow squash (try to use mostly the yellow skin area)
SPECIAL EQUIPMENT: 8 inch oven proof skillet (may use 6 cup muffin tin)

 GEORGE'S TIPS:

You shouldn't even think about eating this without a smattering of trans-fat free margarine.

PREP TIME
5 MINS

COOK TIME
5 MINS

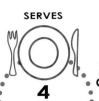
SERVES
4

calories **110**
fat **7g**
protein **3g**
fiber **5g**
net carbs
6

SIMPLY GRILLED VEGETABLES

The name may say it all, but this standard is about the best way a vegetable can end up. Cooking, at its most basic, is all about bringing out flavors through technique. It's no surprise then that just about everything tastes better when it's hot off the grill! It's a technique that's stuck around since, well, just about ever.

directions

1. Preheat a grill to medium high or use an indoor grill top or grill pan over high heat. ·

2. Place all of the cut vegetables on a baking sheet and toss with the olive oil, garlic, basil, salt and pepper.

3. Lay the vegetables flat on the grill and cook for about 2 minutes on each side until nicely marked. Remove from the grill and serve.

shopping list

1 medium zucchini, cut on a bias into 1/4 inch slices

1 medium yellow squash, cut on a bias into 1/4 inch slices

1 medium eggplant, cut into 1/2 inch thick slices

1 portabella mushroom cap, cut into 1/2 inch slices

2 tablespoons olive oil (may also use canola oil)

1 teaspoon fresh chopped garlic

1 tablespoon fresh chopped basil leaves

1/2 teaspoon kosher salt

1/4 teaspoon freshly ground black pepper

GEORGE'S TIPS:

These vegetables make a great side for just about any grilling affair. See a photo of them with *Grilled Chicken Parmesan Casserole* on page: 107.

For perfect grill marks, flip the veggies only once and leave them be as they cook.

calories 90 | fat 8g | protein 4g | fiber 1g | net carbs 3

PREP TIME 15 MINS | COOK TIME 5 MINS | SERVES 4

SCAMPI SAUTEED MUSHROOMS

I always make extra scampi butter and keep it in the freezer and when I'm in a pinch for a quick side or appetizer, there's nothing easier than this! Always a dinner party pleaser, who can deny something scampi?

directions

1. Wipe the mushrooms clean with a damp cloth. Trim any dirty or dried stems and discard.
2. Place 3 tablespoons of the scampi butter in a large sauté pan over medium heat.
3. Add the mushrooms and sauté for 4 or 5 minutes, until the mushrooms are fully cooked.
4. Remove from the heat and quickly stir in the remaining scampi butter. Divide among 4 small plates. Sprinkle the parsley on top and finish with fresh lemon wedges.

shopping list

16 ounces small button mushrooms
5 tablespoons Scampi Butter
2 tablespoons chopped fresh parsley
1 lemon cut into wedges

SCAMPI BUTTER

1/2 cup trans-fat free margarine, or unsalted butter (1 stick), softened
1 tablespoon minced fresh garlic
1 tablespoon minced red onion
1 tablespoon chopped fresh parsley leaves
1/2 teaspoon garlic powder
dash of ground white pepper
dash of Worcestershire sauce
juice of 1 fresh lemon

Scampi Butter

1. In a bowl, whisk together all the ingredients until well blended. It takes a bit of work, but if you keep whisking, it will mix together. (If you have trouble getting the liquid to combine, it may help to soften the butter in the microwave for just a couple seconds.)
2. Spoon the compound butter onto a piece of plastic wrap and form it into a log about 2 inches around. Roll it up like a big cigar and twist the ends shut. You may store in the refrigerator for 1 week or freeze much longer.

 ## GEORGE'S TIPS:

Making scampi butter from a healthy spread like Smart Balance doesn't change the flavor but eliminates all cholesterol and trans fats from the recipe. I say, why not? In fact, it's the only way I prepare this now.

calories 84 | fat 6g | protein 3g | fiber 3g | net carbs 3

PREP TIME 10 MINS | COOK TIME 7 MINS | SERVES 4

veggies / sides

ASPARAGUS, RED PEPPERS AND PINE NUTS

The good thing about asparagus is that it's always going on sale. Sure, the regular price would have you believe that someone figured out how to fuel their vehicle with asparagus fumes, but I'm almost always seeing it "half off" in the grocery ads and on those weeks, we're eatin' good! This classic combo of asparagus, red peppers and pine nuts will fuel your flair for the gourmet, but I haven't quite figured out how to get my car running off it yet.

shopping list

1 pound fresh asparagus ends trimmed

2 tablespoons trans fat free margarine

1 cup red bell pepper strips (about 1 pepper)

1 tablespoon pine nuts

1/4 teaspoon Kosher salt

1/8 teaspoon freshly ground black pepper

directions

1. Place a pot of water over high heat and bring to a boil.

2. Drop the trimmed asparagus into the boiling water and cook for about 3 to 5 minutes depending on the thickness of the stalks until tender but still crisp.

3. While the asparagus is cooking, place the margarine and pepper strips in a large sauté pan over medium heat and cook until tender, just about the time it takes for the asparagus to cook.

4. When the asparagus is done, drain and add them to the sauté pan with the salt and pepper and cook for just another minute and serve.

GEORGE'S TIPS:

Olive oil or canola oil may be used in place of the margarine or you may even use real butter if that's your thing! The pine nuts do have fats and can be omitted or replaced with a different healthy choice such as walnuts or husked sunflower seeds!

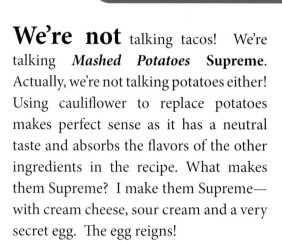

calories 210 | fat 18g | protein 7g | fiber 2g | net carbs **3**

PREP TIME **10 MINS** | COOK TIME **6 MINS** | SERVES **4**

veggies / sides

MOCK MASHED POTATOES SUPREME

We're not talking tacos! We're talking *Mashed Potatoes Supreme*. Actually, we're not talking potatoes either! Using cauliflower to replace potatoes makes perfect sense as it has a neutral taste and absorbs the flavors of the other ingredients in the recipe. What makes them Supreme? I make them Supreme— with cream cheese, sour cream and a very secret egg. The egg reigns!

shopping list ✏

1 medium head cauliflower
3 ounces softened cream cheese
2 tablespoons sour cream
1 egg
1/4 cup grated Parmesan cheese
1/8 teaspoon straight chicken base or boullon (may substitute ½ teaspoon salt)
1/8 teaspoon garlic powder
1/8 teaspoon freshly ground black pepper
1/2 teaspoon chopped fresh or dried chives, for garnish
3 tablespoons trans fat free margarine

directions

1. Bring a large pot of water to a boil over high heat.

2. Clean and cut cauliflower into small pieces. Cook in boiling water for about 6 minutes, until well done.

3. Drain well. Do not let cool. Pat the cooked cauliflower very dry between several layers of paper towels (otherwise the "potatoes" will be too thin and runny).

4. With an immersion blender in a deep bowl or in a food processor, pulse the hot cauliflower with the cream cheese, sour cream, egg, Parmesan, garlic, chicken base, and pepper until almost smooth.

5. Garnish with chives and serve hot with a pat of margarine

🎩 GEORGE'S TIPS:

If you are worried that the cauliflower has cooled down too much to add the raw egg, you can microwave the finished "potatoes" for 30-45 seconds, just to be safe. Low fat or fat free cream cheese, or Neufchatel cheese may be used in place of the cream cheese. Fat free sour cream is another good idea if you are watching fat.

PREP TIME
5 MINS

COOK TIME
10 MINS

SERVES
6

calories **60**
fat **2.5g**
protein **5g**
fiber **3g**
net carbs
3

BROCCOLI POLONAISE

Don't let the name fool you, it's harder to say than it is to make. This tasty French side dish is a perfect example of just how easy cooking can be. It's also a great way to bring leftover broccoli back to the table for seconds!

directions

1. Preheat oven to 375 degrees F.

shopping list ✏

vegetable oil spray

1 pound cooked broccoli spears (frozen or leftovers works perfectly)

2 eggs

3 tablespoons grated Parmesan cheese

1/2 teaspoon kosher salt

1/4 teaspoon freshly ground black pepper

2. Spray an 8 x 8 inch baking pan with vegetable oil spray and place the broccoli inside.

3. Add the remaining ingredients to a bowl and whisk until blended.

4. Slowly pour the mixture over the broccoli spears inside the baking dish and bake for 10 – 12 minutes until they start to brown slightly and the eggs are cooked.

5. Serve with the good stuff that clings to the bottom of the pan.

 GEORGE'S TIPS:

Feel free to go half broccoli, half cauliflower with this. Try it with asparagus too!

calories 82 | fat 4g | protein 8g | fiber 1g | net carbs 4

PREP TIME 10 MINS | COOK TIME 10 MINS | SERVES 6

veggies / sides

SPINACH RICOTTA DUMPLINGS

I first made dumplings with spinach and ricotta in the early 80's when we were trying our hand at California Cuisine in South Florida. They're more interesting than plain 'ole dumplings and healthier to boot! Eat them before a certain "Sailor Man" gets to them.

directions

1. Place a stock pot over medium-high heat, add the chicken stock and bring to a simmer.

2. In a medium bowl, combine the remaining ingredients and mix well with a rubber spatula.

3. Using 2 regular tablespoons drop scant tablespoons of the mixture into the hot stock using one spoon to scrape the mixture off the other. Let dumplings simmer for about ten minutes and serve hot with the broth in small bowls or without the broth on a plate with butter and fresh basil if desired.

shopping list

8 cups chicken stock or soup

1/2 cup whole milk ricotta cheese

1/2 cup chopped cooked spinach, well drained

1 large egg

1/2 cup soy flour (may use whole wheat flour)

1/2 teaspoon kosher salt

1/8 teaspoon garlic powder

1/8 teaspoon freshly ground black pepper

6 fresh basil leaves, optional

 GEORGE'S TIPS:

These dumplings also make a great gourmet appetizer served on small plates smothered in **Tomato Al Fresco Sauce**, recipe on page: 55!

calories 90 | fat 5g | protein 7g | fiber 1g | net carbs 4

PREP TIME **15 MINS**

COOK TIME **25 MINS**

SERVES **12**

veggies / sides

SAVORY GARLIC HERB MUFFINS

These totally gluten free muffins remind me of one of my favorite things; Foccacia bread! They're versatile little fellows that are great griddled with cream cheese for breakfast or served hot with butter for dinner!

directions

1. Preheat the oven to 375 degrees F.

2. Spray the muffin pan with the cooking spray. In a small bowl, mix together two tablespoons soy flour and one tablespoon sugar substitute. Evenly sprinkle each cup of the muffin pan with the mixture, being careful to coat the sides by tilting the pan over the bowl to catch the crumbs.

3. In a larger bowl whisk together the 1 1/2 cups soy flour, 1/3 cup sugar substitute and baking powder. Add the remaining ingredients and whisk until completely blended.

4. Pour the batter into the prepared muffin pan, filling each cup two-thirds of the way and bake for about 20-25 minutes until the tops start to brown and a toothpick inserted in the center comes out clean. Be careful not to overcook or the muffins will be dry.

5. Remove the muffins from the oven and let cool for at least 5 minutes before removing them from the pan. Serve warm. Refrigerate any leftovers in a sealed container.

shopping list

vegetable oil spray

1 1/2 cups plus 2 tablespoon soy flour

1/3 cup plus 1 tablespoon sugar substitute (recommended: Splenda)

1 1/2 teaspoons baking powder

3 large eggs

3/4 cup heavy cream (may use unsweetened soy milk)

1/2 cup club soda

1/4 cup red bell pepper, small diced

1/4 cup green bell pepper, small diced

1 tablespoon fresh basil leaves, chopped

1/4 teaspoon fresh garlic, minced

1/8 teaspoon kosher salt

SPECIAL EQUIPMENT: 12 cup non-stick or silicone muffin pan

 GEORGE'S TIPS:

You gotta have these with a pat of butter, trans-fat free margarine or cream cheese! Also try making a mini sandwich with leftover ham or roast beef.

calories 110
fat 1.5g
protein 4g
fiber 3g
net carbs **17**

PREP TIME **15 MINS**

COOK TIME **75 MINS**

SERVES **8**

veggies / sides

TWICE BAKED CANDIED SWEET POTATOES

At Thanksgiving when I made these for the first time, I was good and only ate one. When I tried them cold on the second day, I ate three more! Turns out that they are just as good, if not better cold as a dessert; they taste just like sweet potato pie! The good news is by replacing marshmallows with meringue and eliminating the added sugars, going overboard won't sink your diet.

directions

1. Preheat the oven to 400 F.

2. Use a fork to poke a few holes in each potato, place them on a sheet pan and bake for about 45 minutes to 1 hour until fairly soft.

3. Add all the meringue ingredients into a mixer bowl and beat on high for about 2-3 minutes until soft peaks form.

shopping list

4 large sweet potatoes, washed

MERINGUE

3 egg whites

1/2 teaspoon vanilla extract, no sugar added

1/4 teaspoon cream of tartar

1/4 cup sugar substitute (recommended: Splenda)

FILLING

2 egg yolks

1/4 cup sugar substitute (recommended: Splenda)

1 teaspoon vanilla extract, no sugar added

1/2 teaspoon pumpkin pie spice

1 tablespoon half and half (or unsweetened soy milk)

1/3 of the total finished meringue

SPECIAL EQUIPMENT: electric mixer and pastry piping bag

4. When the potatoes are done, slice in half and carefully scoop out half of the cooked pulp from each skin into a large bowl, reserving the skin on the sheet pan.

5. Add the filling ingredients to the bowl with the cooked pulp and mix well with a whisk until blended and smooth. (If too thick, a food processor may be used.)

6. Use a rubber spatula to fold 1/3 of the meringue into the potato filling and place the remaining meringue into a pastry bag with a large open tip.

7. Spoon the potato filling evenly into each of the 8 shells and then pipe the meringue in the pastry bag over each from end to end.

8. Place stuffed sweet potatoes back into the oven and bake for about 15 minutes or until the meringue starts to turn golden brown. Remove and serve hot topped with walnuts or pecans if desired.

PREP TIME
15 MINS

COOK TIME
55 MINS

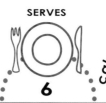
SERVES
6

calories **160**

fat **12g**

protein **8g**

fiber **0g**

net carbs
5

THE HAYDENS' "HASH BROWN" CASSEROLE
recipe by Stacy and Mark Hayden

Mark is a moderator of the forums at StellaStyle.com and we had the pleasure of driving cross country together on the way to a get-together of many forum friends! We had a blast and I don't think there was one second that wasn't filled with intriguing conversation! Then I met his lovely wife Stacy on the way home and realized that it's true what they say, especially in this case: behind every great man is a great woman! This, Stacy's spaghetti squash take on a hashbrown casserole is not only good, it's a hands down favorite of our forum members.

shopping list

vegetable oil spray

1 medium spaghetti squash

1 1/2 cups shredded cheddar cheese

2 tablespoons finely chopped yellow onion

1/4 cup sour cream

1/4 teaspoon salt, more or less to taste

1/8 teaspoon black pepper, more or less to taste

SPECIAL EQUIPMENT: 8 x 6 inch oven proof glass baking dish or pie pan

directions

1. Cut spaghetti squash in half, clean out seeds and place face down in 1 1/2 inches of water in a glass baking dish. Cover tightly with plastic wrap and microwave on high for 10-12 minutes. Meanwhile, pre-heat oven to 350 degrees F.

2. After cooked, remove the strands of meat from the squash with a fork and put into a bowl with all the ingredients and mix well to combine.

3. Spray the casserole dish with vegetable oil, then place the mixture in evenly and bake for about 50 minutes. Remove and let cool for 5 minutes before serving.

 ## STACY AND MARK'S TIPS:

This recipe is great as a side dish for any meal but we often enjoy the leftovers with some bacon and eggs in the morning... kind of reminds us of Cracker Barrel.

Nine Foods for the Top of Your List

I was going to do a list of ten great foods, but the tenth would just be the very obvious, but no less important, skinless chicken breast… you just can't say anything bad about a perfect and *perfectly lean* protein!

1. Broccoli

- - - > Low in calories and carbohydrates, broccoli is a simple and natural way to get the fiber your body needs. It's also packing a good amount of vitamin C, without all of the sugars of citrus! I prefer my broccoli a little firm, which is a good thing because overcooking broccoli can eliminate a lot of its supposed immune system strengthening compounds.

2. Almonds

- - - > Though they may seem to be high in fat, almonds are loaded with the "good" monounsaturated fat that can lower your cholesterol. Add to that their extremely high fiber content and copious amounts of skin-friendly vitamin E and you can see why we love baking with almond flour. Plus, almond flour just gives our baked goods an extra rich flavor you can't even get with white flour. Think about it… they make marzipan from these little wonders for a reason!

3. Spinach

- - - > Make that salad a spinach salad, you won't regret it! Though most of the famous iron in spinach isn't absorbed into your body, it's still a wonderful source of anti-aging antioxidants and even fiber.

4. Cauliflower

- - - > Although it comes from the same (cabbage) family as broccoli and shares most of the same, and very good, nutritional characteristics; cauliflower is indispensable in the Stella kitchen for its chameleon like abilities! Whether you're mashing it into "mashed potatoes" or grating it into "rice", your old favorite white foods have never been so healthy.

5. Salmon - - - > The king of Omega-3 foods, this stuff can ward off all kinds of health problems, including heart disease. Smoked, baked or grilled, we just love it and it shows… in our healthier looking skin!

6. Cantaloupe - - - > A great dessert or breakfast alternative, you can get all the potassium of a banana and antioxidants like vitamin C and beta carotene. Hey, who knows what else this super fruit can do for you, moldy cantaloupes used to be the best source of penicillin!

7. Walnuts - - - > Sure, they're chock full of fiber, but walnuts are also a wonderful and fish-free source of Omega-3 fatty acids! Ever tried to snack on a handful of salmon at the office? If you have, we'd love to see video of it. We'll watch it with a tub of walnuts!

8. Fresh Berries - - - > Blueberries, Raspberries, Cranberries… they all have one thing in common; health benefits! Antioxidants that improve memory, aging and can even prevent infection are all included. We always garnish our desserts with fresh berries for just this reason! Well, also because they're really good.

9. Apples - - - > As a breakfast or snack, the pectin in apples can actually lower your glucose levels even though they do have their own natural sugars. With a lower glucose level, you'll stay full and satisfied longer.

vegetarian entrees

SPAGHETTI SQUASH LO MEIN

DIRTY CAULIFLOWER "RICE" AND
BLACK SOY BEANS

SESAME GARLIC EGGPLANT STIR FRY

SUMMER SQUASH PARMESAN

vegetarian

calories 110 | fat 9g | protein 1g | fiber 0g

net carbs 6

PREP TIME **10 MINS**

COOK TIME **30 MINS**

SERVES **8**

SPAGHETTI SQUASH LO MEIN

Spaghetti squash lends itself perfectly to lo mein, delivering all the flavors, without all the carbs. You don't get a fortune cookie at the end of your meal, so here's a fortune: EXPECT GREAT LEFTOVERS IN YOUR FUTURE!

directions

1. Cook the spaghetti squash by cutting in half length wise, scraping away the seeds from the center, and boiling the two halves in a large pot for around 20 to 25 minutes, until the pulp pulls away in strands with a fork.

shopping list

1 medium spaghetti squash
1 tablespoon canola oil
1/4 cup sesame oil
1 clove fresh garlic, thinly sliced
1/2 cup teriyaki sauce (not thick marinade)
1/2 teaspoon salt
1/2 teaspoon freshly ground black pepper
1/4 teaspoon garlic powder
sesame seeds as garnish
SPECIAL EQUIPMENT: wok or large sauté pan and 12 quart stock pot

2. Place a wok or large sauté pan over high heat with the canola and sesame oil. Add the fresh sliced garlic and cook for just a few seconds to lightly brown the garlic.

3. Use a fork to remove the cooked spaghetti squash in strands and add to the hot pan cooking for about 2 minutes while stirring or tossing carefully.

4. Remove from heat and serve garnished with sesame seeds if desired.

 # GEORGE'S TIPS:

Add mushrooms, bean sprouts and bell peppers for a Low Mein feast or serve as is alongside *Tilapia Tempura*, recipe page: 141.

calories 105 | fat 6g | protein 7g | fiber 5g | net carbs 3

PREP TIME **15 MINS** COOK TIME **8 MINS** SERVES **8**

vegetarian

DIRTY CAULIFLOWER "RICE" AND BLACK SOY BEANS

"Dirty" is a Cajun cooking term for throwing tons of herbs and everything except the kitchen sink into a dish. If you *were* to throw in the *actual* kitchen sink, the term would change to *"Sinky"*, though I have not actually attempted such a ridiculous technique. (Mostly because it does not exist.)

directions

1. Grate the fresh cauliflower head as you would cheese, using the largest holes of a cheese grater. A food processor with a grating blade is easiest for this.

2. Heat the butter and oil in an extra large skillet over medium-high heat. Add the onions, garlic and shredded cauliflower and cook for 2 minutes while stirring.

shopping list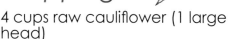

4 cups raw cauliflower (1 large head)
1 tablespoon unsalted butter or trans-fat free maragarine
1 tablespoon olive oil
4 tablespoons yellow onion, minced
1/2 teaspoon fresh garlic, minced
2 cups vegetable broth (may use chicken or beef)
1 1/2 cups frozen chopped spinach, thawed and drained
15 ounce can black soy beans, drained and rinsed (recommended: Eden brand)
1 tablespoon fresh parsley, chopped
2 bay leaves
1 teaspoon cumin
1 teaspoon chili powder
1 teaspoon kosher salt
1/4 teaspoon freshly ground black pepper
SPECIAL EQUIPMENT: extra large fry pan or wok

3. Next add the vegetable stock, spinach, black soy beans and seasonings and simmer for about 9 minutes until tender, stirring occasionally. Serve hot.

 # GEORGE'S TIPS:

Do not overcook or the "rice" will turn to mush. If the Cauliflower does not absorb all the liquid simply strain it or serve with a slotted spoon leaving excess broth behind.

calories 125 | fat 12g | protein 1g | **net carbs 2** | fiber 2g

PREP TIME **15 MINS**

COOK TIME **5 MINS**

SERVES **6**

vegetarian

SESAME GARLIC EGGPLANT STIR FRY

We love eggplants and stir frys at the Stella household and usually I make them with teriyaki sauce, but not this time. It turns out I really like this way best; with only sesame oil imparting a deep roasted Asian flavor!

directions

1. Prepare the vegetables and measure the ingredients so you are ready to stir fry very quickly.

2. Place a wok or large sauté pan over high heat with the canola oil until almost smoking hot. Add the red onion, pepper strips and garlic and cook for just a few seconds.

shopping list

2 tablespoons canola oil
1/4 cup thinly sliced red onion
1/3 cup roasted red pepper strips
2 small cloves fresh garlic, chopped
1 large eggplant, cut into 1 inch chunks (about 4 cups)
1 cup sliced bok choy
1/2 teaspoon salt
1/4 teaspoon freshly ground black pepper
1/4 teaspoon garlic powder
1/8 teaspoon crushed red pepper flakes
1 teaspoon sesame seeds
3 tablespoons sesame oil
SPECIAL EQUIPMENT: wok or large sauté pan

3. While stirring constantly add the eggplant, bok choy and salt and cook for about 2 minutes more.

4. Stir in the remaining ingredients, cook for another 2 minutes and serve.

 # GEORGE'S TIPS:

If you don't have any bok choy I use chopped romaine lettuce all the time as a "cheat" that only you will know!

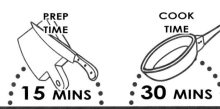

PREP TIME **15 MINS** COOK TIME **30 MINS** SERVES **8**

calories 130 | fat 9g | protein 6g | fiber 2g

net carbs 4

SUMMER SQUASH PARMESAN

Rachel got the idea for this "lasagna style" recipe when our organic garden was being overrun by giant, almost canoe sized zucchini and yellow squash. This was our favorite recipe to come out of our monster squash season; of course we've had to adjust things a bit for the average sized squash that they sell in supermarkets. The ones that you can't hollow out and paddle down a river.

directions

1. Preheat oven to 350 degrees F. and spray an 8 x 8 inch baking dish with vegetable oil.

2. Heat the olive oil in a large sauté pan until almost smoking hot. Add the zucchini, squash and spices and cook until lightly browned and tender, only about 3 minutes. Drain.

3. Next add the lightly cooked squash saute to the bottom of the baking dish and cover with the tomato slices.

4. Add all the ricotta filling ingredients to a bowl except the Parmesan cheese and mix well.

5. Spread the ricotta filling over the layer of tomato slices and sprinkle the Parmesan cheese over all.

6. Bake for 30 minutes or until the Parmesan cheese turns a golden brown and the squash is very tender and hot throughout. Cool for 5-7 minutes before slicing to serve.

shopping list

2 vine ripe tomatoes cut into 1/4 inch slices

SQUASH SAUTE
2 tablespoons extra virgin olive oil
2 medium zucchini cut into 1/4 inch slices
2 medium yellow squash cut into 1/4 inch slices
1 teaspoon kosher salt
1 teaspoon dry oregano
1/2 teaspoon fresh chopped garlic
1/4 teaspoons freshly ground black pepper

RICOTTA FILLING
1/2 cup whole milk ricotta cheese (may use low fat)
1/2 cup sour cream (may use low fat or plain yogurt)
1/2 teaspoon kosher salt
1/2 teaspoon dry oregano
1/8 teaspoon garlic powder
1/8 teaspoon freshly ground black pepper
1/2 cup grated Parmesan cheese

SPECIAL EQUIPMENT: 8 x 8 inch baking dish

poultry

GRILLED CHICKEN PARMESAN CASSEROLE

HOLIDAY ROAST TURKEY BREAST

CHICKEN MARSALA

MOROCCAN CHICKEN SKILLET

MOJO BAKED CHICKEN

CHEESY GROUND TURKEY
"ONE SKILLET" HELPER

CHICKEN CACCIATORE

AUNT FRAN'S FAVORITE FAMILY CASSEROLE

CHICKEN FRANCAIS

"CRAZY WOMAN" BILLIE'S
SMOTHERED CHICKEN

calories 685 · fat 42g · protein 59g · fiber 6g · net carbs **11**

PREP TIME **20 MINS** · COOK TIME **25 MINS** · SERVES **4**

GRILLED CHICKEN PARMESAN CASSEROLE

This grilled version of chicken Parmesan, a Stella family comfort food, is not only fun to make but without the breading and deep frying it's healthier for you too!

directions

1. Preheat the oven to 350 degrees F. and set the grill to medium high or use an indoor grill top or grill pan over high heat.

2. Place all the ingredients except the sauce, cheese, grilled vegetables and garnish in a large ovenproof casserole baking dish and toss with the chicken until each piece is well coated.

3. Grill the chicken on one side for about 4 minutes until browned and grill marks appear, then turn and cook for only a couple more minutes on the other side. (The chicken will not be completely cooked yet.)

4. Place the grilled vegetables into the bottom of the casserole dish followed by the partially cooked chicken breasts and top all with *Tomato Al Fresco Sauce*, the sliced fresh mozzarella cheese and whole fresh basil leaves.

5. Bake casserole for about 25 minutes until chicken is thoroughly cooked and cheese is bubbly hot. Serve.

shopping list

2 tablespoons olive oil (may use canola)
2 tablespoons diced red onion
1 teaspoon fresh chopped garlic
1 tablespoon fresh chopped basil leaves
1 teaspoon dry oregano
1 teaspoon kosher salt
1/2 teaspoon freshly ground black pepper
4 boneless, skinless chicken breast halves (about 1 1/4 pounds)
1 batch **Tomato Al Fresco Sauce**, recipe page: 55
8 ounces fresh mozzarella cheese in 4 thick slices
1 batch **Simply Grilled Vegetables**, recipe page: 82
4 large whole fresh basil leaves for garnish

 ## GEORGE'S TIPS:

A *Wilted Spinach Salad with Walnuts and Apples*, recipe page: 65, makes a great start to this healthy family meal.

PREP TIME
10 MINS

COOK TIME
2 HRS 30 MINS

SERVES
12

calories **350**
fat **10g**
protein **55g**
fiber **0g**
net carbs 0

HOLIDAY ROAST TURKEY BREAST

I have always thought that we need to prepare turkey more often throughout the year as it's easy to cook, provides good value for the food dollar and just tastes good! I liked this unconventionally seasoned "Flavors of the Holidays" version the first time I made it as a chef at the Grand Floridian Resort in Walt Disney World where everyday seems like a holiday! Sooo… why not declare today a Holiday in your house?

directions

1. Preheat oven to 325 degrees F. Lightly coat the pan with vegetable spray.

2. To make a spice rub, place all the ingredients except the turkey into a medium size bowl and mix well.

shopping list

vegetable oil spray
3 tablespoons canola oil
1 teaspoon kosher salt
1/2 teaspoon cinnamon
1/4 teaspoon freshly ground black pepper
1/4 teaspoon ground ginger
1/4 teaspoon ground allspice
1/4 teaspoon ground nutmeg
4 teaspoons sugar substitute, recommended: Splenda
a 5 to 7 pound turkey breast, bone-in
SPECIAL EQUIPMENT: ovenproof 10 inch chicken fryer pan or shallow roasting pan

3. Place the turkey breast upright in the pan and use your hands to coat evenly with the rub.

4. Roast the turkey breast uncovered until it starts to turn golden brown. Loosely tent the breast with aluminum foil and finish cooking until a meat thermometer inserted in the thickest part registers 185 F. or about 2 1/2 hours total cooking time. When done, remove from the oven and let stand for 10 minutes before carving.

 GEORGE'S TIPS:

Rather than carve a turkey as it sits, we chefs prefer to remove the entire 2 breast halves off the bone and then slice them from top to bottom at an angle (against the grain) on a cutting board for perfect slices every time!

calories 490 | fat 24g | protein 59g | fiber 1g | net carbs 5

PREP TIME **15 MINS**

COOK TIME **20 MINS**

SERVES **4**

poultry

CHICKEN MARSALA

Whether you just want a quick stove top dinner that just happens to be gourmet or a dish that can feed the masses at parties; Chicken Marsala is a true time tested favorite of all!

directions

1. Place the oil in a large non stick sauté pan over high heat until almost smoking hot.

2. Dredge the chicken cutlets first in the seasoned soy flour, then the eggs and add to the hot pan. Cook for about 3 minutes on each side until golden brown and almost fully cooked; remove and set aside.

3. Using the same pan add the trans-fat free margarine, onions, garlic and mushrooms and cook for about 2 minutes.

4. Next add the beef base, Marsala, heavy cream, pepper and parsley and cook on high heat for about 4 more minutes until liquid is reduced by about half.

5. Add the cooked chicken cutlets back into the pan with the sauce and continue cooking for about 4 more minutes until sauce thickens by about half again. Remove chicken from pan and spoon sauce and mushrooms over the top to serve.

shopping list

2 tablespoons canola oil (may use olive oil)

1 1/2 pounds boneless skinless chicken breast cut or pounded into 4 thin cutlets.

1 cup soy flour, seasoned with 1/2 teaspoon kosher salt and 1/4 teaspoon black pepper in a medium bowl

3 eggs, beaten in a medium bowl

1 tablespoon trans-fat free margarine

2 tablespoons diced red onion

1 small clove finely minced garlic

10 ounces Crimini or "Baby Bella" mushrooms

1 teaspoon beef base (may use 2 beef bouillon cubes)

3 ounces Cream Marsala wine

6 ounces heavy cream

1/4 teaspoon freshly ground black pepper

1 tablespoon fresh chopped parsley

GEORGE'S TIPS:

Serve a simple **Tomato Fromage**, recipe page: 79, with this dish for a colorful and delicious accompaniment!

calories 340 | fat 13g | protein 36g | fiber 4g | net carbs 17

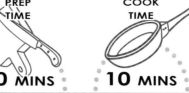

PREP TIME 20 MINS | COOK TIME 10 MINS | SERVES 4

poultry

MOROCCAN CHICKEN SKILLET

Cinnamon, tumeric, and cayenne are proven to be of 3 of the healthiest spices of life! They provide typical flavors predominant to festive Moroccan food, food that is abundant in fruit and vivid earthy flavors! Your family won't be complaining about having chicken again as chicken doesn't have to be boring and this hearty recipe proves it!

directions

1. Heat the oil in a large skillet over medium-high heat and add the chicken, onion and garlic and cook, turning occasionally until browned, about 2 minutes.

2. Mix the dry seasonings together in a bowl, sprinkle over the chicken and cook for another 2 minutes.

3. Add the remaining ingredients and simmer covered for 5 to 6 minutes and serve.

shopping list

1 tablespoon olive oil
1 pound boneless, skinless chicken thighs, cut into large chunks
1/2 cup sliced red onion
2 small cloves minced fresh garlic
1/2 teaspoon salt
1/2 teaspoon paprika
1/4 teaspoon ground cumin
1/4 teaspoon ground cinnamon
1/4 teaspoon ground tumeric
1/8 teaspoon cayenne pepper
1 cup yellow squash, half-moon sliced
1 cup zucchini, half-moon sliced
1/2 cup roasted red peppers, julienne cut
1 cup chicken broth
1/2 cup fresh figs, large diced (may use dry figs or prunes)

 # GEORGE'S TIPS:

Try using whole boneless, skinless chicken breasts or chunk boneless pork loin in place of the chicken thighs for a nice change! You can cut out most of the net carbs by eliminating the figs, but hey, figs are definitely good for you.

PREP TIME
15 MINS

COOK TIME
2 HRS 15 MINS

SERVES
4

calories **533** | fat **25g** | protein **66g** | fiber **1g**
net carbs 2

MOJO BAKED CHICKEN

Growing up as a chef in south Florida in the 70's, a favorite staple in our kitchens (and still ours today) was a Cuban marinade; "Mojo Criollo" ceremoniously used during a traditional whole pig roast. We used this flavorful and tangy marinade for everything and as this recipe will prove, it's especially effective for gettin' on your chicken Mojo too!

directions

1. Preheat oven to 350 degrees F. Lightly coat a roasting pan with vegetable spray.

2. Place the chicken halves skin side up in the roasting pan, pour the dressing and lime juice over them and sprinkle each piece evenly with the remaining ingredients.

3. Cover the pan tightly with aluminum foil and bake for 1 hour.

4. Remove the chicken from the oven and baste with the drippings. Continue baking uncovered until well browned, about 1 hour and 15 minutes more, basting every 20 minutes until meat is falling off the bones.

shopping list

vegetable oil spray

1 whole chicken (about 4 pounds), cut in half

8 ounces no-sugar added Italian dressing (may use Mojo Criollo marinade found in the International foods isle)

2 tablespoons lime juice

1 teaspoon kosher salt

1/2 teaspoon freshly ground black pepper

1/2 teaspoon garlic powder

2 tablespoons chopped fresh cilantro

4 bay leaves

1 teaspoon paprika

SPECIAL EQUIPMENT: 1 medium roasting pan

GEORGE'S TIPS:

For extra crispy skin, place the pan of baked chicken under the broiler for a couple minutes to finish. This is a great main course to enjoy with a heaping serving of Dirty Cauliflower Rice and Soy Black Beans, recipe page: 101.

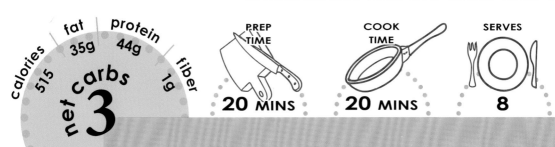

calories 515 | fat 35g | protein 44g | fiber 1g | net carbs 3

PREP TIME **20 MINS** | COOK TIME **20 MINS** | SERVES **8**

CHEESY GROUND TURKEY "ONE SKILLET" HELPER

Who doesn't remember when Hamburger Helper was all the rage! My Mom was a great chef but we must have had every kind of "Helper" there was at least once a week! And now I realize that even chefs need a break and it's a no-brainer to throw everything into a single pan and serve the family dinner from that very same pan just minutes later!

directions

1. Heat the oil in a large skillet over medium-high heat. Add the celery, onions and peppers and cook until slightly tender.

2. Add the ground turkey and cook until browned. If there is any excess fat, drain off with a spoon.

3. Next add the mushrooms, garlic, and seasonings and simmer for 4 to 5 minutes, stirring constantly.

4. Remove from the heat, stir in the cheddar cheese, sour cream and cream cheese and serve garnished with fresh chopped parsley if desired.

shopping list

2 tablespoons canola oil
2 cups chopped celery
1/2 cup chopped red onion
1/2 cup chopped red bell pepper, may use roasted in a jar
2 1/2 pounds ground turkey
8 ounces sliced white button mushrooms, may use Crimini or Baby Bellas
1/4 teaspoon minced fresh garlic
1 tablespoon chili powder
1 1/2 teaspoons salt
1/4 teaspoon freshly ground black pepper
1/8 teaspoon garlic powder
1 cup shredded cheddar cheese
1/2 cup sour cream
4 ounces cream cheese, cut into small pieces
1 tablespoon fresh chopped parsley, optional for garnish

GEORGE'S TIPS:

For a delightfully different twist on this skillet use diced eggplant in place of the celery! You can crisp up the skillet by adding another 1/4 cup of cheddar cheese on top and place close under the broiler for just a minute or so until lightly browned!

calories 590 | fat 24g | protein 68g | fiber 3g

net carbs **6**

PREP TIME **15 MINS**

COOK TIME **2 HRS 15 MINS**

SERVES **4**

poultry

CHICKEN CACCIATORE

This family-style version of chicken cacciatore is a little different as it was devised when I took leftover family style chicken, added tomato sauce and peppers and re-baked. In the process I discovered an easy all-in-one way to make a healthier chicken cacciatore by eliminating the traditional extra step of dredging the chicken in white flour and pan browning.

directions

1. Preheat oven to 350 degrees F. Lightly coat a roasting pan with vegetable spray.

2. Pour the *Tomato Al Fresco Sauce* into the roasting pan, place the chicken pieces skin side up into the sauce and sprinkle each piece evenly with the dry spices. (Reserve the bell peppers and onions to add later.)

shopping list ✏

vegetable oil spray
1 batch **Tomato Al Fresco Sauce**, recipe page: 55
1 chicken, cut into 8 pieces (may use chicken leg quarters or any chicken pieces)
1 teaspoon kosher salt
1/2 teaspoon ground black pepper
1/2 teaspoon garlic powder
1/2 teaspoon poultry seasoning
1/2 teaspoon dried oregano
4 bay leaves
1 green bell pepper, seeded and large cut
1 red bell pepper, seeded and large cut
1/2 cup red onion, large chopped
chopped parsley, optional for garnish
SPECIAL EQUIPMENT: medium roasting pan

3. Cover the pan tightly with aluminum foil and bake for 1 hour.

4. Remove the chicken from the oven and add the bell peppers and onions. Continue baking uncovered until well browned, about 1 hour and 15 minutes more, until meat is falling off the bones. Serve with sauce over the chicken and sprinkled with fresh chopped parsley if desired.

 ## GEORGE'S TIPS:

Add small whole button mushrooms or green beans for a heartier meal and a few ounces of red wine will take it up yet another level!

PREP TIME

20 MINS

COOK TIME

50 MINS

SERVES

8

calories **480** | fat **32g** | protein **36g** | fiber **1g**

net carbs **8**

AUNT FRAN'S FAVORITE FAMILY CASSEROLE
recipe by Aunt Fran and Dinah Moore

Self proclaimed "Dingie Dinah" as she is affectionately known on our forums at StellaStyle.com has become a close friend over the many years she has spent helping others on the website and everywhere she goes. Dinah says about her recipe, "This really was a family favorite for decades. Aunt Fran will be tickled if it's included; She's 82 years old and still kicking high! (I love my aunt Fran, can you tell?)"

directions

1. Cut spaghetti squash in half, clean out seeds and place face down in 1 1/2 inches of water in a glass baking dish. Cover tightly with plastic wrap and microwave on high for 10-12 minutes. Meanwhile pre-heat oven to 350 degrees F.

2. Cool cooked squash under cold water, remove the strands of meat from the squash with a fork, put into a large bowl and set aside.

shopping list

4 cups cooked spaghetti squash, about 1 medium squash

1 tablespoon butter, may use butter alternative

1 tablespoon extra virgin olive oil

3/4 cup sliced bell peppers, any color

3/4 cup sliced onions

1/2 cup celery

8 ounces pimentos, drained and sliced or diced

8 ounces canned mushrooms, may use 10 ounces fresh sliced

2 cups cheddar cheese, shredded

8 ounces cream cheese

1 cup half and half cream, may use unsweetened soy milk

vegetable oil spray

1 1/2 pounds cooked boneless skinless chicken breast halves

SPECIAL EQUIPMENT: 9 x 13 inch oven proof glass baking dish or similar

3. Add the butter and olive oil to a sauté pan over medium-high heat and cook the peppers, onions, celery, pimentos and mushrooms until tender-crisp and add to the bowl with the cooked spaghetti squash.

4. Place a saucepan over medium heat and add the half and half, cream cheese and only one cup of the cheddar cheese and heat just until melted. Stir with a whisk to blend, remove and pour over the spaghetti squash and vegetables mixture and toss.

5. Spray the baking dish with vegetable oil and line the bottom with the cooked chicken breast halves. Pour the spaghetti squash sauce mixture over the chicken, top all with the remaining 1 cup cheddar cheese and bake at 350 F for about 50 minutes. Remove and let cool for 5 minutes before serving.

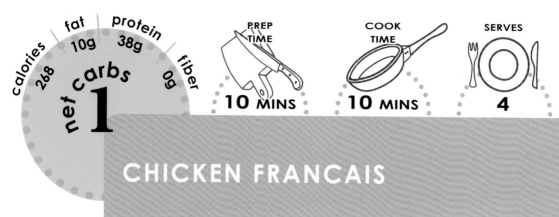

calories 268 | fat 10g | protein 38g | fiber 0g

net carbs **1**

PREP TIME **10 MINS**

COOK TIME **10 MINS**

SERVES **4**

poultry

CHICKEN FRANCAIS

Francais is as classical as cooking gets! This recipe employs the easy and basic technique of sautéing to create the simple classic French beurre blanc or wine and butter reduction sauce. This very same recipe may be used to make fish or veal and is often the basis for many more recipes. Such as if you add capers and green olives it becomes "Picatta".

directions

1. Add the eggs to a medium size bowl and beat well.

2. Place the 4 chicken cutlets into the bowl with the eggs.

3. Reserve 1 tablespoon of the trans-fat free margarine and heat the other tablespoon in a large sauté pan over high heat until almost smoking hot. Adding just a teaspoon of olive oil to the butter substitute will allow for a hotter pan without burning.

4. Add in the egg coated chicken cutlets one at a time, season with salt and pepper over all and cook on 1 side for about 2 to 3 minutes until golden brown.

5. Using tongs, flip each piece over, add the lemon juice, wine, onions, garlic and parsley and continue to cook for 3 minutes more until the chicken is thoroughly cooked. If liquid runs out add more white wine or stock to keep cooking.

6. Remove from heat, stir in the reserved 1 tablespoon of margarine and serve immediately. Garnish with fresh lemon wedges and parsley if desired.

shopping list

2 eggs
1 pound boneless skinless chicken breast, cut into 4 thin cutlets
2 tablespoons trans-fat free margarine
1/2 teaspoon kosher salt
1/8 teaspoon freshly ground black pepper
2 tablespoons fresh lemon juice (about 1 lemon)
2 tablespoons dry white wine (use your favorite and drink the rest with dinner!)
1 tablespoon finely chopped red onion
1 tablespoon chopped fresh parsley
1/4 teaspoon minced fresh garlic (about 1/2 small clove)

 ## GEORGE'S TIPS:

You may lighten up the fats and calories in this recipe by using only egg whites or Egg Beaters egg substitute and the wine may be substituted with chicken or vegetable stock.

PREP TIME
10 MINS

COOK TIME
25 MINS

SERVES
5

calories 870 / fat 50g / protein 86g / fiber 0g
net carbs 13

"CRAZY WOMAN" BILLIE'S SMOTHERED CHICKEN
recipe by Billie Willis

Billie Willis or "Crazywoman" has been a part of our extended family of friends on our forums at StellaStyle.com for as long as I can remember. Just post on the forums you are new and Crazywoman will be one of the first of many to come to welcome you with links and info! When I asked for recipes from the forum Billie replied: "I'm not a very inventive cook, but I made this one up because I wanted something different to serve visiting family." Well Billie, you must be crazy if you think this recipe is not inventive! It's also good.

directions

1. Add the water, garlic powder, Creole seasoning, onion powder and chicken thighs to a pressure cooker and cook at high for about 10 minutes until cooked. Let the pressure release naturally.

shopping list
2 cups water
3/4 teaspoon garlic powder
1/2 teaspoon creole seasoning
1/4 teaspoon onion powder
3 pounds or 10 chicken thighs, fresh or frozen if pressure cooking
1/4 cup Ranch dressing
1 cup mayonnaise
4 oz cream cheese, softened to room temperature
2 tablespoons fresh chopped onions
1 tablespoon parsley flakes, freeze-dried, dry or fresh
1/4 teaspoon paprika
1 cup shredded Colby-jack cheese, may use cheese of your choice
SPECIAL EQUIPMENT: pressure cooker or crock pot

2. Preheat oven to 350 F. and when chicken is done transfer to a casserole dish.

3. In a small bowl mix together the Ranch dressing, mayo, cream cheese, onions, parsley and paprika until well blended. (A wand blender works well for this.)

4. Pour mixture over the chicken, sprinkle with shredded cheese and bake for about 15 minutes until cheese starts to brown. Serve hot.

 ## BILLIE'S TIPS:

If you do not have a pressure cooker the chicken may be boiled until thoroughly cooked then make the casserole and bake. For a crock pot just put the raw thawed chicken and all the ingredients except the Colby-jack cheese in and cook for 4-5 hours on high. Then place the cooked chicken in a casserole dish, top with the cheese and bake.

meats

BLACKENED PORK CHOPS

STUFFED MEATLOAF MINIS

STEAK DIANE

ITALIAN PORKETTA

HAM "MOCK MAC" AND
CHEESE CASSEROLE

KANSAS CITY DRY RUB RIBS

GORGONZOLA BEEF TENDERLOIN

PORK LOIN FLORENTINE

FEARLESS ROAST RACK OF LAMB WITH
ROASTED VEGETABLES

COUNTRY FRIED STEAK WITH WHITE GRAVY

calories 370 | fat 28g | protein 25g | fiber 0g | net carbs 0

PREP TIME 5 MINS | COOK TIME 8 MINS | SERVES 4

meats

BLACKENED PORK CHOPS

Blackening anything is a quick and easy way to make a memorable meal. Pork chops, in particular are one of my favorite things to give a little Cajun kick! In eight minutes, you can be eating these chops before your oven would even preheat for the old, run of the mill, breaded pork chops. I've always said that carbs will slow you down!

shopping list

1 pound pork chops, 4 chops about 4 ounces each and less than 1 inch thick

2 tablespoons **Blackening Spice**, recipe page: 57

4 sprigs fresh cilantro, optional for garnish

directions

1. Turn your overhead exhaust fan on and place the oil in a large cast-iron skillet or heavy pan over high heat until almost smoking hot.

2. Season both sides of the pork chops liberally with the blackening spice, place in the skillet and cook for about 3 or 4 minutes on each side until well seared and cooked through. Serve garnished with fresh cilantro if desired.

GEORGE'S TIPS:

These Cajun chops go perfect accompanied by collards or spinach with roasted peppers; just add a jar of red pepper strips, butter, salt and pepper to a bag of frozen collards or spinach and microwave!

calories 370 | fat 17g | protein 48g | fiber 0g

net carbs **3**

PREP TIME
30 MINS

COOK TIME
75 MINS

SERVES
8

meats

STUFFED MEATLOAF MINIS

Restaurants today are in a back to basics mode and comfort foods from the past have never been more "IN"! This is definitely one way to present an old favorite with a new twist. Besides, who doesn't love stuffed anything?

directions

1. Preheat oven to 350° F. In a large bowl, mix together the beef, eggs and everything except the pepper strips, ham and mozzarella.

2. Use 1/2 the meat mixture to equally line the bottom of all 8 sections of the mini loaf pan.

3. Next place equal amounts of the strips of peppers, ham and cheese into the center of each compartment and press into the bottom layer of meat mixture.

shopping list

2 pounds ground chuck (may use mixed ground meats)
2 large eggs
1/2 cup grated Parmesan cheese
1/4 cup small diced red onion
2 tablespoons chopped fresh parsley leaves
2 small cloves garlic, minced
1/2 teaspoon dried oregano
1/2 teaspoon dried basil
1 teaspoon kosher salt
1/2 teaspoon ground black pepper
1/2 cup roasted red bell pepper strips
4 ounces baked ham, cut into strips
8 ounces fresh whole mozzarella cheese, cut into strips (may use sliced or shredded)
SPECIAL EQUIPMENT: 8 compartment mini loaf pan

4. Cover each section of the pan with the remaining beef mixture and press down lightly, sealing the fillings in as best as possible.

5. Bake for about 25 minutes, or until the temperature on a meat thermometer registers 165° F. Drain fat and serve.

 # GEORGE'S TIPS:

A very lean ground beef, such as ground sirloin can be used to limit fats. You can even try ground turkey, though the more expensive ground turkey, from all breast meat has a tendency to dry out.

PREP TIME

10 MINS

COOK TIME

10 MINS

SERVES

4

calories 390 | fat 27g | protein 35g | fiber 1g

net carbs 2

STEAK DIANE

This classic French dish uses a traditional cream reduction to thicken the sauce instead of cornstarch. It really is a quite simple gourmet dish and a real comfort food for me that was usually prepared tableside in restaurants waaay back in the 70's.

directions

1. Place the oil in a large sauté pan over high heat until almost smoking.

2. Season both sides of the beef tenderloins with salt, pepper and garlic powder and add to the hot pan with the diced onions.

shopping list

1 1/2 lbs beef tenderloin (trimmed of all fat)
2 tbsp vegetable oil
1 portabella mushroom
2 tbsp finely chopped red onion
4 oz button mushrooms
1 cup heavy cream
1 oz Marsala wine
1 tbsp no sugar added low sodium beef base
1/8 teaspoon black pepper
1/8 teaspoon garlic powder
2 tbsp fresh chopped parsley
1 tbsp butter or substitute
salt, pepper and garlic powder to season

3. Flip the tenderloins once. When the tenderloins are seared, but not yet fully cooked, remove from pan and set aside.

4. Add heavy cream, beef base, black pepper, and garlic powder. Stir as the sauce reduces down and thickens. Add the button mushrooms and wine. Continue to stir.

5. Add the tenderloins back to the pan. Season a sliced portabella with salt and pepper and add it to the pan.

6. Cook until the liquid reduces and thickens. Add the parsley.

7. Remove from heat and stir cold butter into sauce to thicken further. Serve over vegetables.

 GEORGE'S TIPS:

Chicken can be used instead of beef to create a dish similar to Chicken Marsala.

calories 260 | fat 10g | protein 37g | fiber 0g

net carbs 2

PREP TIME **10 MINS**

COOK TIME **60 MINS**

SERVES **8**

meats

ITALIAN PORKETTA

We simply love going to Italian festivals where you are pretty much guaranteed to find a smorgasbord of great eats! Porketta is almost a given to be on the menu, as sure as Gyro at a Greek festival. A slow roasted, tender pork loin, Porketta is sliced thin and full of Italian flavors that I'm positive you will never forget!

shopping list
2 pounds boneless pork loin
3 tablespoons dill seed
1 tablespoon fennel seed
1/4 teaspoon oregano
1/4 teaspoon basil
1 teaspoon freshly ground black pepper
1/4 teaspoon garlic powder
1/4 teaspoon onion powder

directions

1. Heat oven to 350 degrees F. Combine seasonings together and coat roast with mixture.

2. Place pork in a roasting pan and bake for about 45 minutes to 1 hour, until internal temperature reads 150 degrees F.

3. Let cool for 10 minutes and slice very thin to serve.

GEORGE'S TIPS:

Have your own Italian festival, starting with my *Antipasta on a Stick*, recipe page: 47.

fat 16g | **protein** 8g | **calories** 210 | **net carbs** 4 | **fiber** 3g

meats

PREP TIME	COOK TIME	SERVES
15 MINS	20 MINS	8

HAM "MOCK MAC" AND CHEESE CASSEROLE

With this recipe I am revisiting an old favorite my Mother used to make for me. Casseroles are not only true comfort foods but a great way to use leftovers and get the most for your dinner dollar as this filling casserole turns a side dish into the main course!

directions

1. Place the rack in the center position and preheat the oven to 375 degrees F. Bring a large pot of water to a boil and season with salt. Spray the casserole dish with vegetable oil.

2. Cook the cauliflower in the boiling water for about 5 minutes until crisp yet tender. Drain well, pat between layers of paper towels to dry and transfer to the baking dish.

3. Bring the cream to a simmer in a small saucepan and whisk in the cream cheese, mustard, salt, pepper and garlic until smooth.

4. Stir in 1 1/2 cups of the cheese and whisk for just a minute until the cheese melts. Remove from the heat and pour into the casserole dish, covering the cauliflower.

5. Sprinkle the cubed ham over all, top with the remaining 1/2 cup cheese and bake for about 15 minutes until browned and bubbly hot. Let cool for a bout 5 minutes and serve.

shopping list

vegetable oil spray
kosher salt for water
1 large head cauliflower, cut into small florets and pieces
3/4 cup heavy cream (may use unsweetened soy milk, recommended: Silk brand)
4 ounces cream cheese, cut into small pieces (may use low-fat)
1 1/2 teaspoons Dijon mustard
1/2 teaspoon kosher salt
1/4 teaspoon ground black pepper
1/8 teaspoon garlic powder
1 1/2 cups shredded cheddar cheese, plus 1/2 cup more for topping the casserole
6 ounces baked ham, cubed
SPECIAL EQUIPMENT: 8 x 8 inch oven-proof casserole dish

GEORGE'S TIPS:

Although I suggest using the leftovers from a ham dinner to make this casserole, packages of fully cooked, cubed ham are available in the meat department of grocery stores sold above the baked hams.

calories 610 | fat 42g | protein 53g | fiber 0g | net carbs **1**

PREP TIME **20** MINS | COOK TIME **130** MINS | SERVES **8**

meats

KANSAS CITY DRY RUB RIBS

There are many varieties and ways of making BBQ ribs and people take them seriously, so let me tell you a secret about my recipe, in case you take yours seriously. The "Kansas City" name only pertains to the fact that these succulent ribs simply remind me of the flavor of the old KC Masterpiece potato chips I used to eat! Do they make these ribs in Kansas City? Couldn't tell you, but I can tell you they sure do taste good!

directions

1. Spray the sheet pan with vegetable oil, place the rack in the center position and preheat the oven to 290 F.

shopping list

vegetable oil spray
1/4 cup canola oil
2 tablespoons kosher salt
2 tablespoons paprika
1 1/2 teaspoons freshly ground black pepper
2 teaspoons garlic powder
2 teaspoons onion powder
2 tablespoons sugar substitute (recommended: Splenda)
1 tablespoon liquid smoke
3-4 pounds pork spareribs (2 large racks)
SPECIAL EQUIPMENT: 1/2 size sheet pan or baking dish

2. Place all the ingredients except ribs into a bowl and mix with a fork until a mud like consistency. Rub this mixture liberally over all the ribs, concentrating on the meaty side.

3. Place the rubbed ribs meaty side up on the sheet pan and cover tightly with aluminum foil. Bake for 2 hours or until ribs easily pull apart.

4. Remove, strain and reserve any liquid. To finish, grill the ribs for about 5 minutes on each side or place under the broiler on high until they start to crisp. Then pour reserved rib liquid over ribs before serving hot.

GEORGE'S TIPS:

Try the rub created in this recipe on other cuts of meat, such as brisket or even chicken breast!

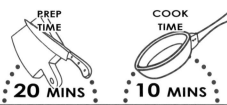

PREP TIME **20 MINS** COOK TIME **10 MINS** SERVES **3**

calories **810** net carbs **5** fat **60g** protein **53g** fiber **0g**

GORGONZOLA BEEF TENDERLOIN

While apprenticing under French chefs as a young man it was common to put blue cheese and butter on top of hot steaks just before serving, so it would be melting as it gets to the table. This naturally low carb recipe plays off of that concept and does it well!

directions

1. Place oil and butter in a large sauté pan over high heat until almost smoking hot.

2. Season both sides of the tenderloin medallions with salt and pepper and add to the hot pan.

3. Add in the onions and garlic and continue to sear the beef for about 2 minutes.

shopping list

1 tablespoon vegetable oil (recommended: canola)
1 tablespoon unsalted butter
1 pound beef tenderloin, cut into six medallions
1/4 teaspoon kosher salt
1/4 teaspoon ground black pepper
2 tablespoons chopped red onion
1/4 teaspoon chopped garlic
1 1/2 ounces red wine
1 1/2 ounces red wine
GORGONZOLA SAUCE
2/3 cup sour cream
1/3 cup heavy mayonnaise
4 ounces Gorgonzola blue cheese, crumbled
1 1/2 teaspoons Worcestershire sauce

4. Next turn the medallions over, cook for about 1 minute and sizzle with the red wine. Cook just until liquid is reduced, about two minutes more and remove from heat and serve with warm Gorgonzola sauce.

Gorgonzola Sauce

1. Combine the sour cream, mayonnaise, blue cheese and Worcestershire in a saucepan over low heat for just a couple minutes and serve with sautéed tenderloin medallions.

 # GEORGE'S TIPS:

Try grilling the tenderloins or even chicken breast along with Portobella mushroom caps before smothering with the Gorgonzola sauce!

Calories 300 | **fat** 15g | **protein** 35g | **fiber** 0g

net carbs 3

PREP TIME 20 MINS

COOK TIME 60 MINS

SERVES 12

meats

PORK LOIN FLORENTINE

This wonderful stuffed pork loin roast has become a favorite in the Stella household and rightfully so! Whole 12-15 pound loins go on sale all the time. You can get three or more great family meals from just one pork loin and save a ton of dough!

directions

1. Preheat oven to 350 degrees F.

2. Add the filling ingredients to a bowl, mix well and set aside.

3. Using a long chef's knife, carefully filet the pork loin open flat by slicing lengthwise a 1/2 inch up from the bottom of the roast. If the loin does not lay flat after filleting, simply make a shallow slice where it is thickest and press down with the palm of your hand to flatten.

4. Place the filleted pork loin on an oil coated sheet pan, spread the filling evenly over all and top with the spinach leaves.

shopping list

2 cups fresh spinach leaves

FILLING
2 cups part skim ricotta cheese
1/2 cup grated Parmesan cheese
1 large egg
1/2 teaspoon fresh chopped garlic
1/2 teaspoon garlic powder
1/2 teaspoon dry oregano
1 tablespoon fresh chopped basil (may use 1/2 teaspoon dry basil)
1/4 teaspoon freshly ground black pepper
1/2 cup roasted red pepper strips

PORK LOIN
4 pounds boneless pork loin, trimmed
2 ounces olive oil
2 teaspoons kosher salt
1 teaspoon fresh chopped garlic
1/2 teaspoon garlic powder
1/2 teaspoon dry oregano
1 tablespoon fresh chopped basil (may use 1/2 teaspoon dry basil)
1/2 teaspoon ground black pepper
SPECIAL EQUIPMENT: baking twine

5. Roll the stuffed loin up being careful to keep pushing the filling back in. Wrap the twine around the center about every 2 inches along the length of the roast making a knot after each time. Then wrap the twine from end to end a couple times and tie off.

6. Bake the stuffed pork loin for about 1 hour until a meat thermometer inserted in the thickest part reads 150 degrees F. Let rest for about 5 to 10 minutes before cutting off the strings and cut the roast into 1/2 inch thick slices to serve.

calories 340
fat 21g
protein 29g
fiber 3g
net carbs 7

PREP TIME **15 MINS**

COOK TIME **45 MINS**

SERVES **4**

meats

FEARLESS ROAST RACK OF LAMB WITH ROASTED VEGETABLES

A rack of lamb certainly isn't something you buy everyday on your way home from work. It is usually encased in heavy plastic, not so familiar and well, just a bit daunting. I can tell you right now, go ahead and pick one up and see how SIMPLE and EXCITING any night of the week can be when you're eating Stella Style!

directions

1. Preheat the oven to 450 degrees F. Place the oil in a sauté pan over high heat until almost smoking hot.

2. Season both sides of the rack of lamb with the salt, pepper and garlic powder and place the whole rack meaty side down in the hot pan.

3. Let cook for about 3-5 minutes on one side only until meat is well seared.

4. Place the lamb rack seared side up on a small sheet pan or roasting pan and bake until a meat thermometer stuck in the thickest part of the roast reads 140 degrees F for a perfect rare, about 30 minutes. Let sit for 5 minutes and then slice in between each bone to make individual chops and serve garnished with fresh mint if desired.

shopping list

ROAST RACK OF LAMB
1 tablespoon extra virgin olive oil
2 pound average whole rack of lamb, fat cap removed and trimmed
1 teaspoon kosher salt
1/2 teaspoon ground black pepper
1/4 teaspoon garlic powder
4 sprigs fresh mint, optional for garnish

ROASTED VEGETABLES
vegetable oil spray
3 ribs celery, cut into thirds
2 medium yellow squash, halved crosswise
2 medium zucchini, halved crosswise
1 medium yellow onion, quartered
1 red bell pepper, cored, seeded, and quartered
1 clove garlic, minced
2 tablespoons olive oil
1 1/2 teaspoons kosher salt
1 teaspoon dried oregano
1 teaspoon paprika
1/4 teaspoon ground black pepper
1/8 teaspoon garlic powder

Roasted Vegetables

1. Spray a roasting pan with vegetable oil and preheat oven to 350 degrees F. or just cook the roasted vegetables right in the roast rack of lamb pan at 450 degrees with the lamb on top.

2. Toss all of the ingredients including the cut vegetables in a large bowl.

3. Arrange vegetables in the roasting pan and bake for about 35-40 minutes (or until the lamb is done, if roasting with the lamb) until well done.

calories 400
fat 27g
protein 35g
fiber 4g
net carbs 7

PREP TIME: 15 MINS
COOK TIME: 10 MINS
SERVES: 4

meats

COUNTRY FRIED STEAK
WITH WHITE GRAVY

Growing up in the South, fried anything is good to me! Until Rachel and I did some traveling by car this year, I had plum forgotten about this classic greasy spoon dish that's a staple in truck stops and diners. As soon as we returned home I had to reinvent it so I could take that journey down food memory lane!

directions

1. Place a deep heavy pan or pot over medium-high heat and fill with at least 1 inch vegetable oil. Heat the oil to 350 degrees F; it's important to monitor and maintain the temperature or the breading and oil will burn.

2. In a medium bowl, whisk the eggs and water to make an egg wash.

3. In a larger bowl, mix the breading ingredients together.

4. Working over a cutting board, use a meat tenderizing mallet and pound each 1/4 inch medallion of beef on both sides until almost flat. Place the beef between 2 layers of plastic wrap to prevent the meat from sticking to the mallet or cutting board.

shopping list

3-6 cups vegetable oil (depending on pot size)
2 large eggs
2 tablespoons water
1 pound Top Round or Top Sirloin beef (trimmed of all outside fat and cut into 4 equal size medallions about 1/4 inch thick each)
SPECIAL EQUIPMENT: meat tenderizing mallet
BREADING
2 1/3 cups soy flour
2 teaspoons salt
1 teaspoon ground black pepper
1 teaspoon garlic powder
WHITE GRAVY
1/2 cup heavy cream
1/2 cup chicken stock
1/4 teaspoon salt
1/4 teaspoon ground black pepper
1/8 teaspoon garlic powder
2 tablespoons sour cream

5. Dip each piece of pounded steak into the breading, then the egg wash, and then back into the breading again, making sure to coat well.

6. Pat off any excess breading and carefully place each piece in the hot oil. Fry until golden brown and crisp on the outside, only about 4 minutes. Depending on how much oil used, you may need to turn the pieces over in the oil after 2 minutes to cook evenly all the way around.

7. Remove cooked steaks with tongs or a slotted metal spatula and place on paper towels for a couple minutes to drain excess oil before serving smothered with white gravy.

White Gravy

1. Add all the ingredients except sour cream to a large surface sauté pan and cook over high heat for 4 to 5 minutes, stirring constantly with a high heat rubber spatula until sauce is reduced by about a third.

2. Remove pan from heat, stir in the sour cream until well blended and serve immediately.

Stella Style on a Budget

There's no denying that food prices are going up, up and up. In the short term, it's devastating many a grocery budget and in the long term, there's no telling the impact this can have on our overall health. More and more families are being pushed into low priced and high calorie convenience (junk) food just to get by, but it shouldn't and doesn't have to be like that. Here are a few ways you can save a few without gaining a few... inches on your waistline.

Shop Around
If you have two, three or even more grocery chains in your area, invest in a plastic cooler so that you can hop from store to store picking up sale items without your cold food warming up.

Map Things Out
We like to sit down every week and plan many of our meals around the weekly grocery store ads. Think of it like the show Iron Chef, where you have a few set ingredients (the fresh foods with the best sale prices) and you have to mix and match them to make recipes.

Keep It Simple
The best meals are made with the fewest ingredients, it's a fact (I say it is!). Simplify your favorites for savings.

Go Fresh AND Frozen
I've been known to go crazy and throw eight kinds of vegetables into a stir fry, from time to time—but at two or three dollars a veggie, that can add up. Try buying fresh green veggies like broccoli or green beans and an inexpensive, frozen bag of stir fry vegetables from the freezer aisle to fill in the blanks. You'll have all of the variety, while still retaining the natural vitamins of a fresh veggie.

Find the Right Time to Buy Bulk

If you've ever shopped at one of those "club" stores, you know that buying in bulk can add up rather quickly. If it's food that could spoil before you've finished it or if it's food that you're likely to snack, snack, snack on; you'd be better off paying slightly more for a smaller package. Now, if it's chicken breasts on sale for half price, buy them up and stick em' in the freezer!

Pack the Protein

Buying breakfasts, lunches and snacks that pack the most protein for the buck will help you get through your day feeling full and satisfied. Eggs, nuts, beans and soy or vegetable proteins are all relatively cheap for the amount of protein you'll get.

Plan on Leftovers

There's something to be said about elegantly executed leftovers. Some dishes, like casseroles, even taste better when you've let the flavors mingle overnight. We're almost always eating last night's dinner for lunch, so when it comes to our shopping list, we've got lunch covered.

Buy Reduced Produce

You'd be surprised by what you can find on the produce section's reduced rack. Grocery stores aren't trying to sell you rotten fruit and vegetables, just RIPE ones at ridiculously cheap prices. Sure, you'll have to eat them within a day or two, but every penny counts and you were going to buy something for dinner anyway, weren't you?

Get a Subtotal

Next time you're shopping, keep all of your non-food items separate and ask for a subtotal before ringing up the food. You may be surprised by how much of your grocery budget is going to household items and toiletries. In the end, your health is worth any cost and switching to generic toiletries, cleaners, detergents and the like may save you more money you can put on the dinner table.

seafood

TILAPIA TEMPURA

SEA SCALLOPS PROVENCAL

BALTIMORE BAKED STUFFED SHRIMP

MUSSELS FRA DIAVOLO

ROASTED PESTO SALMON

TILAPIA PARMESAN

calories 325
fat 24g
protein 23g
fiber 1g
net carbs **4**

PREP TIME **15 MINS**
COOK TIME **15 MINS**
SERVES **6**

seafood

TILAPIA TEMPURA

A great adaptation of an Asian classic that has really become an American comfort food in our family! This recipe is easy and always comes out perfect with no fuss or muss and it's low carb to boot. A little Tilapia goes a long way in this healthy recipe providing a lot of bang for the shopping budget buck!

directions

1. Place a pot over medium-high heat filled with at least 2 inches of vegetable oil and heat to 350 degrees F.

2. Make the Tempura Batter by whisking all the ingredients together in a bowl until smooth. (If too thick add just a little water to thin until mud consistency.)

shopping list

4 to 6 cups vegetable oil (more or less depending on the pot used)
1 lb fresh tilapia fillets (cut into 12 equal pieces)
TEMPURA BATTER
1 cup soy flour
3/4 cup club soda
2 large eggs
1/2 teaspoon salt
1/8 teaspoon freshly ground black pepper
1/8 teaspoon garlic powder
1 tablespoon canola oil
SPECIAL EQUIPMENT: 2 quart or larger saucepan or portable tabletop deep fryer

3. Using your fingers dip each piece of tilapia into the batter one at a time, shake off excess on the inside of the bowl and slowly "ease" the coated fish into the hot oil and release. You should be able to cook only 2 or 3 pieces at the same time repeating the process until all the fish is cooked. (Do not overfill the pan and be careful that the pan is deep enough or the hot oil could boil over as it rises when you place in the fish.)

4. Cook each filet for about 4 minutes flipping over once, until golden brown. Remove and let sit on paper towels to drain excess oil before serving immediately with malt vinegar or tartar sauce if desired.

 GEORGE'S TIPS:

Try this low carb tempura batter for everything from shrimp to mushrooms! It's especially perfect served accompanied by *Spaghetti Squash Lo Mein*, recipe page: 99.

PREP TIME
15 MINS

COOK TIME
8 MINS

SERVES
4

calories 150
fat 5g
protein 20g
fiber 1g
net carbs 5

SEA SCALLOPS PROVENCAL

I first made this recipe almost 30 years ago while working as a chef in Ft. Lauderdale, Florida right after Rachel and I got married. It truly is a comfort food for me because those were great and exciting times for young chefs. I've always loved scallops and they're very low in calories and have a ton of protein too!

directions

1. Heat the oil in a large heavy sauté pan or iron skillet over high heat until almost smoking hot.

2. Season the scallops well with the salt and pepper and place gently in the hot pan. Sear on the first side for about 3 minutes and then individually gently turn scallops over.

3. Squeeze the half lemon over the scallops and add the onions, garlic, tomatoes, basil and trans-fat free margarine and cook it all for about 3 minutes more.

4. Stir in the soy milk, and cook for 2 minutes more to reduce. Serve in a shallow rimmed bowl by its lonesome or over spaghetti squash garnished with fresh basil leaves.

shopping list

1 tablespoon extra virgin olive oil

1 pound large fresh sea scallops (frozen is not recommended)

1 teaspoon kosher salt

1/4 teaspoon freshly ground black pepper

1/2 fresh lemon, squeezed

2 tablespoons chopped red onion

1/2 teaspoon chopped fresh garlic

1 cup diced tomatoes

2 tablespoons chopped fresh basil

2 tablespoons trans-fat free margarine

3 tablespoons unsweetened soy milk, recommended: Silk brand

GEORGE'S TIPS:

Try this recipe using shrimp or use BOTH!

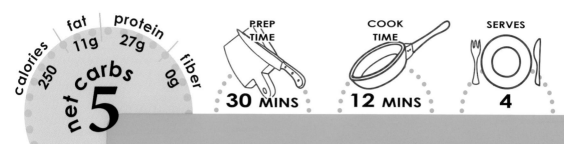

calories 250 | fat 11g | protein 27g | fiber 0g

net carbs 5

PREP TIME **30 MINS**

COOK TIME **12 MINS**

SERVES **4**

BALTIMORE BAKED STUFFED SHRIMP

Maryland means blue crabs and blue crabs by law must be served or cooked with Old Bay seasoning. At least that's how I learned it from my Mom on the trips up and down the Eastern seaboard where my parents would be sure to stop and let us try whatever food the area was known for! Sure there were pecans and slow-cooked BBQ in Georgia, ham in Virginia but Maryland blue crabs were always my mother's favorite!

directions

1. Preheat the oven to 375 degrees F and coat a baking dish or skillet with vegetable oil.

2. In a large bowl, mix all the stuffing ingredients together until blended. Make 12 equal balls from the mix and set aside.

3. Lay each shrimp flat and vein side down in the coated baking dish and place a ball of stuffing on top of each. Wrap the tail up over the stuffing and press it slightly into the stuffing so it will hold its shape.

4. Drizzle the shrimp with the melted butter, wine, and lemon juice and season lightly with salt and pepper. Bake for about 10-12 minutes, or until the shrimp are tender and just cooked. Serve basted in the juices and garnished with lemon and parsley if desired.

shopping list

vegetable oil spray
1/2 pound raw jumbo shrimp, minimum 12 pieces, peeled and deveined with tail on.
2 tablespoons melted unsalted butter
1 ounce dry white wine
1 teaspoon fresh lemon juice
1/4 teaspoon kosher salt
1/8 teaspoon ground black pepper
1 lemon, cut into wedges, optional for garnish

CRAB STUFFING

1 pound blue crabmeat, but may use claw meat or lump available in a can or plastic tub in your grocery store seafood department
1 tablespoon small diced red bell pepper
1 tablespoon small diced green bell pepper
1 tablespoon finely chopped fresh parsley leaves and few sprigs extra for garnish
1 tablespoon heavy mayonnaise
2 eggs
1 tablespoon baking powder
1 tablespoon Worcestershire sauce
1 1/2 teaspoons Old Bay seasoning

SPECIAL EQUIPMENT: 9 x 13 inch casserole dish or 10 inch ovenproof skillet

calories **195** | fat **8g** | protein **19g** | fiber **1g**

net carbs **8**

PREP TIME **15 MINS** | COOK TIME **7 MINS** | SERVES **6**

seafood

MUSSELS FRA DIAVOLO

Simple, sweet, succulent, spicy, and good… Need I say more? Mussels are inexpensive compared to most shellfish, you get more of them per pound than clams or oysters and they can be found in almost every seafood department nowadays. They are great as an appetizer or perfect as an entree and always ready in just a few minutes. Even the cooked leftovers can be made into a cold marinated salad!

shopping list

2 tablespoons olive oil
1/2 cup chopped red onion
1 tablespoon fresh chopped garlic
1 1/2 cups chopped plum tomatoes
2 tablespoons chopped fresh basil and 4 whole sprigs more for garnish
1/2 teaspoon cayenne pepper
1/2 teaspoon salt
1/4 teaspoon freshly ground black pepper
2 pounds fresh mussels, washed and debearded
2 ounces red wine
SPECIAL EQUIPMENT: Large sauté or sauce pan or small stock pot with fitting lid

directions

1. Heat olive oil in a large pan over medium high heat. Add onions, garlic tomatoes, basil, cayenne, salt and pepper and cook for just a minute.

2. Add the cleaned mussels to the pan and pour the wine over all.

3. Cover tightly and cook only about 4 or 5 minutes until the mussels begin to open. (Any mussels that do not open should be discarded) Serve in large soup bowls or on a platter with liquid from the bottom of the pan poured over the mussels and garnish with fresh whole basil.

 ## GEORGE'S TIPS:

Add assorted shellfish and more of a full fledge marinara sauce and this recipe becomes another one of my favorites, "Zuppa De Pesche." Serve it over spaghetti squash!

seafood

calories 660
fat 54g
protein 41g
fiber 0g
net carbs 1

PREP TIME 10 MINS
COOK TIME 15 MINS
SERVES 4

ROASTED PESTO SALMON

Rachel and I have always liked salmon but when we found out that the omega-3 fatty acids and potassium in it actually help to make your skin look younger we liked it all the more! This unusual salmon dish made with a classic sauce was first suggested to me by Dan Cohen, the producer of the first season of my Food Network show, Low Carb and Lovin' It. Well, it's been a few years and many salmon recipes later and we've finally taken Dan up on his suggestion, but because of the salmon we still look like it was just yesterday!

shopping list

vegetable oil spray
1 1/2 pounds boneless, skinless salmon filet, cut into 4 equal pieces
BASIL PESTO
2 cups fresh basil leaves, packed (save a few leaves for garnish if desired)
1/2 cup extra virgin olive oil
3 tablespoons pine nuts (Toast in a dry skillet over medium heat until lightly browned, may use roasted shelled sunflower seeds or peanuts in a pinch)
1 small fresh garlic clove (about 1/2 teaspoon chopped)
1/4 teaspoon kosher salt
1/4 teaspoon freshly ground black pepper
1/4 cup grated Parmesan cheese
SPECIAL EQUIPMENT: 1/2 size non-stick sheet pan and food processor

directions

1. Preheat the oven to 375 degrees F. Spray a sheet pan with vegetable oil spray and set aside.

2. Place all the pesto ingredients into a food processor and pulse on high until almost a puree.

3. Place the salmon pieces on the sheet pan, smear the top of each evenly with a thin coating of pesto and bake for approximately15 minutes. (The thickness of the salmon fillets may vary; thin pieces will cook faster.) Serve garnished with fresh basil leaves if desired.

 ## GEORGE'S TIPS:

If you have any leftover pesto you can keep it refrigerated for a few days or freeze it indefinitely. Of course you can use it up by trying it on chicken breast or even to season a healthy spaghetti squash pasta!

PREP
TIME
15 MINS

COOK
TIME
15 MINS

SERVES
2

calories 295 · fat 18g · protein 26g · fiber 0g
net carbs **4**

seafood

BAKED TILAPIA PARMESAN

What can I say about tilapia that I haven't already said? That's that actual question I just asked Rachel as I sit here late at night writing and trying to figure out what to say about a great, yet simple dish I have been making for years. Rachel didn't have any ideas either, so… THIS IS GOOD. EAT BAKED TILAPIA PARMESAN. This is the last sentence I have to write before I can get some sleep!

directions

1. Preheat the oven to 375 degrees F and coat a baking dish with vegetable oil.

2. Place the tilapia filets in the baking dish and drizzle with the wine and lemon juice.

shopping list ✎

vegetable oil spray

8 ounces tilapia fillets (filet of sole or orange roughy may be used)

1 ounce white wine, recommended: Chablis, chardonnay or pinot grigio

2 teaspoons fresh lemon juice

1/4 cup grated Parmesan cheese

1 tablespoon mayonnaise

2 tablespoons softened butter, may use butter alternative

1 tablespoon green onions, finely chopped

1/4 teaspoon salt

1/8 teaspoon freshly ground black pepper

1/8 teaspoon dried oregano

2 lemon wedges for garnish, if desired

3. Add the remaining ingredients to a medium bowl and mix well. Top the fish with even amounts of the mixture and bake for about 15 minutes, or until the tilapia starts to brown. Serve basted in the juices and garnished with lemon if desired.

 GEORGE'S TIPS:

You can make this recipe simpler and "lighter" by cooking the tilapia with wine, butter, lemon, salt and pepper and leave off the rest!

148

snacks

EASY CINNAMON CRISPS

INSTANT PEANUT BUTTER FUDGE TRUFFLES

MONTE CARLO LETTUCE WRAPS

PAN FRIED PIZZA CHEESE

GINNY'S CAJUN SPICED WALNUTS

STRAWBERRY YOGURT POPS

calories 70 | fat 6g | protein 3g | fiber 1g

net carbs **2**

PREP TIME **2 HRS**

COOK TIME **15 MINS**

SERVES **8**

snacks

EASY CINNAMON CRISPS

These graham-y treats might remind your kids of a certain box of "Teddy" snack crackers. Don't know what I'm getting at? Just give them a try, they're certain to break the crunchy sweet blues!

directions

1. In a bowl whisk together the almond flour, 1/4 cup sugar substitute, salt, and 1/2 teaspoon of ground cinnamon.

2. Add egg white and vanilla extract to dry ingredients and mix well with a wooden spoon.

3. Place on large sheet of plastic wrap and wrap loosely. Shape into a 1" wide log, round or square, about 7" long. Wrap plastic wrap tightly and refrigerate for 2 hours or overnight.

4. Preheat oven to 350°F and line a sheet pan with parchment paper.

5. Remove log from refrigerator. Unwrap plastic wrap and slice the log into around 24 even pieces. Lay pieces out on sheet pan, evenly spaced.

6. Sprinkle each crisp evenly with a mixture of 1 teaspoon sugar substitute and 1/8 teaspoon cinnamon and bake for 15 minutes or until crispy. Cool and serve or store on the counter in a covered container for up to 3 days.

shopping list

1 cup almond flour, recipe
1/4 cup sugar substitute (recommended: Splenda)
1/8 teaspoon salt
1/2 teaspoon ground cinnamon
1 egg white
1/2 teaspoon vanilla extract, no sugar added
1 teaspoon sugar substitute, for top
1/8 teaspoon ground cinnamon, for top

GEORGE'S TIPS:

Dip into some *Fresh Raspberry Fruit Dip*, recipe page: 58, for an even greater treat!

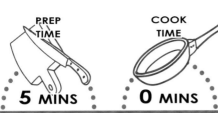

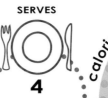 

calories 120 • fat 9g • protein 4g • fiber 1g

net carbs 4

snacks

INSTANT PEANUT BUTTER FUDGE TRUFFLES

One night, I was mixing things up like a mad scientist, trying to make a quick late night snack that would duplicate the taste of a peanut butter cheesecake. What happened next was a complete surprise as the mixture instantly thickened up like fudge! I am certain a food technologist could describe the reaction that causes this quick emulsification, but who cares, its guilt-free fudge and you can make it right now with no waiting, so what are you waiting for?

directions

1. Add the peanut butter, ricotta, sugar substitute and vanilla to a bowl and mix vigorously with a fork for only a minute or so until the mixture thickens considerably and looks like dough.

2. Using 2 small bowls, mix together the cocoa powder and sugar substitute in one and the almond flour and sugar substitute in the other.

3. Next use your hands to roll out marble size pieces of the mixture and then toss them in the coating of your choice and serve!

shopping list

4 tablespoons all natural peanut butter

1 tablespoon ricotta cheese (may use sour cream, heavy cream, half and half or unsweetened soy milk)

5 packets sugar substitute (recommended: Splenda)

1 teaspoon vanilla extract, no sugar added

COCOA COATING

1 tablespoon unsweetened cocoa powder

1 packet sugar substitute

ALMOND COATING

1 tablespoon almond flour

1 packet sugar substitute

 ## GEORGE'S TIPS:

Chilling these on a sheet of wax paper in the freezer for five minutes before serving will help them hold their form, though we can never wait!

calories 171 | fat 10g | protein 16g | fiber 0g | net carbs **3**

PREP TIME **10 MINS** COOK TIME **0 MINS** SERVES **4**

snacks

MONTE CARLO LETTUCE WRAPS

I used to make Monte Carlo sandwiches for years and these wraps are my way of reinventing an old favorite. If you know me, I don't do bread but I also refuse to do without! Once you try these easy wraps you'll see that the best part of a sandwich is what's in the middle anyway! Don't forget to get your Kids in the kitchen to help, they love making AND eating these too!

shopping list
4 thin slices cooked turkey breast
4 thin slices baked ham
4 slices Havarti cheese, may use Swiss
4 teaspoons ranch dressing, may use mayonnaise
4 large leaves iceberg lettuce, may use Romaine or Leaf lettuce
SPECIAL EQUIPMENT: toothpicks

directions

1. On a large microwave safe plate make 4 stacks; each with a layer of ham, turkey and cheese. Heat the layered meat and cheese in the microwave for about 30 seconds, just long enough to melt the cheese.

2. Spread 1 teaspoon Ranch dressing on the inside of each leaf of lettuce, top with a stack of heated meat and cheese, roll it up and secure with toothpicks. Repeat to make all 4 wraps.

GEORGE'S TIPS:

Make a warm reuben lettuce wrap with corned beef, swiss and dressing made from mayonnaise with just a dab of tomato paste. You'll get a good crunch from the lettuce, so the sauerkraut is optional!

calories 64 · fat 4.5g · protein 5g · fiber 0g · **net carbs 1**

PREP TIME **5 MINS** · COOK TIME **5 MINS** · SERVES **4**

PAN FRIED PIZZA CHEESE

This five minute, miniature masterpiece is easily thrown together from the leftovers in your cheese drawer! No *kneed* to throw some dough (anywhere but out the window), it's all the taste, without the regret. I promise you, this is the single most tested, and re-tested recipe in the book! Later, when I'm hungry, I think I may test it again.

directions

1. Set the stove burner to medium or number 5 on the dial.

shopping list

1/4 cup shredded mozzarella cheese

1/4 cup shredded provolone cheese

1/8 cup shredded Swiss cheese (or 1 slice)

1/4 teaspoon dry oregano leaves

1/8 teaspoon kosher salt

1/8 teaspoon garlic powder

SPECIAL EQUIPMENT: 8 inch non-stick fry pan

2. Evenly add the 3 cheeses to the center of the pan in a thin layer leaving an inch or so space around the inside so you can flip the fried cheese later.

3. Next sprinkle the cheese evenly with the oregano, salt and garlic powder and place the pan over the heat.

4. Cook the cheese for about 3 minutes until the bottom of the cheese when lifted at the edge to check is a golden dark brown.

5. Carefully flip the fried cheese and cook for an additional 2 minutes. Remove from heat, flip right side up onto a paper towel or napkin to drain excess oil and immediately cut into 8 wedges. Let cool for 5 minutes to crisp before enjoying!

GEORGE'S TIPS:

Low fat cheese may be used to lighten up the fats in this recipe!

calories 390 | fat 37g | protein 16g | net carbs **2** | fiber 4g

PREP TIME **5** MINS

COOK TIME **25** MINS

SERVES **8**

snacks

GINNY'S CAJUN SPICED WALNUTS

This is one of about a hundred recipes my sister Virginia handed me, hand written on scraps of paper of various sizes. I put the stack of recipes next to my various stacks scattered around my house. Organization doesn't seem to run in our genes! Somehow, this recipe found its way to the top of the stacks and now here it is! Savory, without any added fat. Spicy, it doesn't just have fight, it's a knockout!

shopping list

2 large egg whites
2 teaspoons water
1/2 teaspoon salt
1/2 teaspoon garlic powder
1/2 teaspoon chili powder
1/2 teaspoon ground cumin, optional (but I suggest it!)
1/4 teaspoon cayenne pepper
4 cups walnut halves
SPECIAL EQUIPMENT: brown paper bag

directions

1. Preheat the oven to 325 degrees F.

2. Cut a brown paper bag to size and use it to line a cookie sheet. Spray the top surface of the paper heavily with cooking spray.

3. Whisk the egg whites in a bowl until frothy. Add the water, all the seasonings and whisk thoroughly.

4. Add the walnuts to the egg white mixture and toss to coat well.

5. Spread the coated nuts in a single layer on the oil-coated paper and bake for 20 to 25 minutes. Remove and allow to cool before storing non-refrigerated in a sealed container.

GEORGE'S TIPS:

Try this recipe with any of your favorite nuts or mix them up!

PREP TIME
10 MINS

FREEZE TIME
3 HRS

SERVES
6

calories 45 · fat 1g · protein 2g · fiber 1g

net carbs 5

STRAWBERRY YOGURT POPS

The best thing about these cool treats is that they're real food, not just frozen sugar water. Kids will love to make and eat them—adults will love that their lack of added sugar keeps the kids from climbing the walls and ceiling. I swear I almost saw that once, but that was a long, long time ago. Back before I came up with this recipe!

shopping list ✏

2 cups frozen strawberries, no sugar added

1 cup plain yogurt

1 teaspoon vanilla extract

1/4 cup sugar substitute (recommended: Splenda)

SPECIAL EQUIPMENT: food processor, popsicle mold or 6 count muffin pan with paper cup liners and 6 popsicle sticks

directions

1. Add all the ingredients into a food processor and blend on medium speed for just a minute or two until smooth.

2. Pour the mix into the paper lined muffin cups (or popsicle mold) and cover the entire muffin pan tightly with aluminum foil. Use a sharp knife to cut a small slit in the aluminum foil in the center of each filled muffin cup and place a stick into each. Freeze for at least 3 hours until solid, remove foil and paper and serve.

 ## GEORGE'S TIPS:

We like to freeze our own fresh strawberries when they are in season, or on sale, but freezer aisle strawberries work just fine.

beverages

HOT COCOA SUPREME

STRAWBERRIES AND CREAM SMOOTHIES

HOLIDAY EGGNOG

FROZEN STRAWBERRY MARGARITAS

HONEYDEW AND KIWI "GREEN SLIME"
SLUSHEES

calories 53
fat 3g
protein 4.5g
fiber 2g
net carbs 3

PREP TIME
5 MINS

CHILL TIME
5 MINS

SERVES
2

beverages

HOT COCOA SUPREME

Unsweetened cocoa powder is a staple in our cupboard, as it's great for whipping up satisfying and "legal" desserts. The most simple is a satisfying anytime sugar-free hot cocoa. Unsweetened cocoa like our other favorite staple, Bakers unsweetened chocolate is REAL 100% chocolate with 100% of the health benefits you hear that chocolate has! Whereas, store-bought instant cocoa mixes are mostly sugar with very little real chocolate or real chocolate benefits.

shopping list

1 cup unsweetened soy milk, recommended: Silk brand

4 teaspoons (or 2 packets) sugar substitute, recommended: Splenda

2 tablespoons unsweetened cocoa powder

fresh sugar-free whipped cream, optional

SPECIAL EQUIPMENT: small sauce pan

directions

1. Place all the ingredients except whipped cream in a small sauce pan over medium-high heat. Stir while heating for about 5 minutes until almost boiling and serve in a mug with whipped cream on top if desired.

GEORGE'S TIPS:

Water may be used in place of the soy milk for an even lighter yet delicious hot cocoa! And call me weird, but I like this chilled!

PREP TIME
5 MINS

COOK TIME
0 MINS

SERVES
4

calories **53**
fat **1g**
protein **2g**
fiber **2g**
net carbs
7

STRAWBERRIES AND CREAM SMOOTHIES

We burn out blenders around here quicker than light bulbs! Smoothies rule in the Stella household as anytime snacks, dessert or just a refreshingly cool drink to get in the kitchen and make with your kids! My kids used to wake us up making smoothies late at night! When you consider that before that they were grabbing ice cream, junk food and sodas late at night it was a simple fix to just keep a couple bags of "healthy" frozen fruit in the freezer instead!

shopping list 🖉

12 ounces frozen strawberries

1/4 cup sugar substitute, recommended: Splenda

1 cup unsweetened soy milk, recommended: Silk brand

1/2 cup water

1 teaspoon vanilla extract

4 fresh whole strawberries, cut and placed on the rim of the glass, optional as garnish

SPECIAL EQUIPMENT: Blender

directions

1. Blend all the ingredients in a blender until smooth.

 ## GEORGE'S TIPS:

For a creamier smoothie use half and half in place of the soy milk. Freeze any leftovers in a covered container and enjoy as ice cream later!

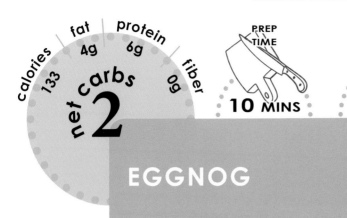

calories 133 | fat 4g | protein 6g | fiber 0g

net carbs 2

PREP TIME **10 MINS**

CHILL TIME **30 MINS**

SERVES **8**

EGGNOG

Winter is a wonderful time for great holiday foods and special little goodies that you just don't see the rest of the year. One such delectable and traditional delight is Eggnog. This version is fun and quick to make while avoiding tons of sugars usually found in store bought versions.

shopping list

6 large eggs

1 cup sugar substitute, recommended: Splenda

1/2 teaspoon vanilla extract

1/4 teaspoon freshly grated nutmeg

2 cups unsweetened soy milk (may use half and half)

1 cup dark rum (may use 1/2 cup Brandy and 1/2 cup dark rum)

SPECIAL EQUIPMENT: Blender (may use a bowl and wire whisk)

directions

1. Place the eggs in the blender on low speed for about 15 seconds until frothy.

2. Add the sugar substitute, vanilla and nutmeg and blend on low for another 15 seconds.

3. With the blender running on low, slowly add the rum and then the unsweetened soy milk. Chill for 30 minutes and serve cold sprinkled with cinnamon or nutmeg.

 GEORGE'S TIPS:

Eggnog is great all by its lonesome so you may leave out the alcohol and simply replace it with another cup of unsweetened soy milk. But for a non-alcoholic twist try adding a cup of chilled coffee instead! Without the alcohol, you'll probably want to make sure you're using pasteurized eggs to be safe, otherwise the alcohol effectively "cooks" everything real good.

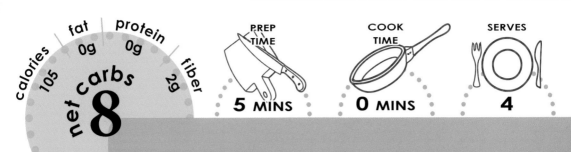

calories 105 | fat 0g | protein 0g | fiber 2g | net carbs 8

PREP TIME **5 MINS** | COOK TIME **0 MINS** | SERVES **4**

beverages

FROZEN STRAWBERRY MARGARITAS

We enjoy barbecues around the pool with family and friends on a lazy (and usually hot in Florida) Sunday afternoon with a cool drink or 2 of course! A cold Margarita on a hot day really fits the bill and puts you in that whole "Margaritaville" mood as "Parrot Heads" know! In fact I think I hear Jimmy Buffet tuning up on the patio and calling my name. "I'll be right there Jimmy and I have the Margaritas!" Oh, it's my dog Reagan barking to take her on a walk.

shopping list

12 ounces frozen strawberries

1 cup sugar substitute, recommend: Splenda

3/4 cup water

4 ounces tequila

1 lemon, juiced

1 lime, juiced

coarse margarita-style salt, optional for glass rims

lemon slices, optional garnish

lime slices, optional garnish

SPECIAL EQUIPMENT: blender and 4 margarita glasses

directions

1. Add all the ingredients except salt and garnish in a blender and blend on high for about 2 minutes until smooth.

2. Rub a lemon slice around the glass rims then dip them in a small plate of salt to coat. Pour the mix into the prepared glasses, and garnish with lemon and lime slices.

GEORGE'S TIPS:

We like to buy fresh strawberries when they are in season and freeze them for making all kinds of drinks!

PREP TIME
5 MINS

COOK TIME
0 MINS

SERVES
4

calories **46**

fat **0g**

protein **.5g**

fiber **1g**

net carbs 11

HONEYDEW AND KIWI "GREEN SLIME" SLUSHEES

Living near Nickelodeon Studios, we used to all go and sit in the audience for filmings of shows like Double Dare and all I can remember was the oceans of "Green Slime". I don't remember much else about that show, but I definitely remember that there were copious amounts of slime. Soooo…as my brain works, when Rachel made these healthy and delicious honeydew delights, without thinking I immediately declared, "They look like 'Slime,'" at which Rachel replied, "Then you don't have to have any!"

shopping list

2 cups fresh honeydew, cubed

1 kiwi, peeled

1/2 cup sugar substitute, recommended: Splenda (use less if fruit is ripe and sweet)

1 cup ice

2 tablespoons fresh lime juice

2 tablespoons fresh lemon juice

4 peeled kiwi slices to place on top of slushees, optional as garnish

SPECIAL EQUIPMENT: Blender or food processor

directions

1. Blend all the ingredients in a blender, pulsing until smooth. Pour into 4 glasses and top with kiwi slices if desired.

 ## GEORGE'S TIPS:

A little vodka turns this into a totally adult drink that will have you saying, "Slime Me"!

desserts

STELLA STYLE CHOCOLATE MARBLE
CHEESECAKE

CHOCOLATE MACADAMIA BARK

CRANBERRY CRISP PIE

FAUX VANILLA ICE CREAM

GINGERBREAD SQUARES WITH
LEMON FROSTING

MOCHA TOFU PARFAITS

FOOL PROOF CHEESECAKE ICE CREAM

SIMPLE QUICK CUSTARD

RICOTTA CARNIVAL FRITTERS

HOLIDAY ALMOND COOKIES

INSTANT STRAWBERRY ICE CREAM

STELLA STYLE NY CHEESECAKE MINIS

ALMOND FLOUR POUND CAKE

calories 317 · fat 29g · protein 9g · fiber 1g · **net carbs 5**

PREP TIME **40 MINS**

COOK TIME **105 MINS**

SERVES **12**

desserts

STELLA STYLE CHOCOLATE MARBLE CHEESECAKE

How do you improve on perfection? Just add gobs of chocolate to Rachel's famous *Stella Style NY Ricotta Cheesecake*, that's how!

directions

1. Place the rack in the center of the oven and preheat to 400 degrees F. Spray the springform pan with vegetable oil spray.

2. Make a water bath so the cheesecake cooks all the way through and the top does not crack too much: Pour about 1 inch of water into a shallow roasting pan big enough to fit the cake pan and place it in the oven on the center rack of the oven to heat.

3. With an electric mixer on low speed, beat the cream cheese, ricotta, sour cream, and sugar substitute for about 1 minute, until well blended only.

4. In a separate bowl, whisk the cream, vanilla, lemon juice, eggs, and egg yolks until blended.

5. Turn the mixer on medium speed and slowly pour the egg mixture into the cream cheese mixture. Beat just until blended: be careful not to overwhip and pour the batter into the greased springform pan.

6. Make the chocolate bark (without the macadamias) and immediately spoon the mixture over the top of the cheesecake and gently swirl it into the cake.

7. Place the pan in the heated water bath. Bake for 15 minutes, and then lower the oven temperature to 275 degrees F. Continue baking for 1 1/2 hours, until the top is lightly golden brown and the cake is pulling away from the sides of the pan. Turn the oven off and leave the cake in the oven to cool down slowly for 2 hours. (Be patient as this keeps the cake tall.) Then remove the cake and refrigerate for at least 3 hours but overnight is best. Cut the cake into 12 slices before serving garnished with fresh sliced strawberries and blueberries and even real fresh whipped cream (Splenda sweetened) if desired.

shopping list

vegetable oil spray
24 ounces cream cheese, softened
1 cup extra-fine ricotta cheese (process in a food processor for 1 minute until smooth)
1/2 cup sour cream
1 1/2 cups Splenda sugar substitute, granulated in bag variety
1/3 cup heavy cream
1 tablespoon vanilla extract
1 Tablespoon fresh lemon juice
2 whole large eggs
3 large egg yolks
1 batch of **Chocolate Macadamia Bark**, recipe on next page (made without the macadamias and made right as the cake is ready for the oven)
SPECIAL EQUIPMENT: food processor, mixer and 8-inch springform pan with outside wrapped tightly in aluminum foil (to keep water bath from getting in the cake)

GEORGE'S TIPS:

It is always a good idea to use an oven thermometer to make certain your oven is at the proper baking temperature to cook the cake evenly.

calories 75 · fat 8g · protein 1.5g · fiber 1.5g

net carbs 2

PREP TIME **10 MINS**

COOK TIME **5 MINS**

SERVES **8**

desserts

CHOCOLATE MACADAMIA BARK

When I first tried to perfect a totally sugar free chocolate I could not seem to get it to harden correctly after adding the bulky sugar substitute….until NOW! I found that the sugar substitute had to be first dissolved into a slurry and THEN and only then will it blend properly with unsweetened chocolate to harden like a real candy bar.

directions

1. Fill a stock pot with 2 inches of water and place over medium high heat to simmer.

shopping list

2 tablespoons butter or alternative

3/4 cup sugar substitute (recommended: Splenda)

2 ounces Baker's brand unsweetened chocolate, chopped (2 squares)

1/4 cup coarsely chopped macadamia nuts (may use almonds, pecans or walnuts)

SPECIAL EQUIPMENT: stock pot, steel bowl that fits on top and a dinner plate lined with aluminum foil

2. Place the bowl over the barely simmering stock pot (do not let boil), add the butter and sugar substitute and mix together with a rubber spatula creating a slurry.

3. Add the chopped unsweetened chocolate and slowly stir for about 2 minutes until just melted and a mud-like consistency. If it thickens too quickly, add a little more half and half.

4. Remove from heat and spread evenly onto the aluminum foil lined plate, sprinkle with chopped nuts and press them into the chocolate. Pop the plate into the freezer for about 10 minutes to harden and then easily remove the chocolate bark from the aluminum foil. Break into pieces and stack back on the plate to serve!

GEORGE'S TIPS:

Trans-fat free margarine such as Smart Balance may be used to lighten up the fats and the sugar substitute may be cut in half for a dark chocolate taste!

PREP TIME

15 MINS

COOK TIME

45 MINS

SERVES

8

calories **100**

fat **7g**

protein **3g**

fiber **3g**

net carbs **6**

desserts

CRANBERRY CRISP PIE

It's a cookie, it's a Pie, it's a… it's hard to say what it is except phenomenally good and easy to make! The crispy cookie topping is to die for and the tart cranberries are a refreshingly different contrast that makes you say "Mmmm"! Be careful, as trying to figure out just what this new taste sensation is all about can easily lead to eating about two thirds of a whole pie in the name of research and development; I should know!

directions

shopping list

vegetable oil spray

12 ounces fresh cranberries, rinsed and patted dry

2/3 cup sugar substitute and 1/2 cup more (recommended: Splenda)

1/2 cup chopped walnuts

1 large egg (may use 2 egg whites)

1/2 cup almond flour

1/8 teaspoon salt (pinch)

SPECIAL EQUIPMENT: 10 inch deep dish pie pan

1. Preheat the oven to 325 degrees F and spray a 10 inch deep dish pie pan with vegetable oil spray.

2. Place the rinsed and dried cranberries into the pie pan and sprinkle with 2/3 cup sugar substitute and the chopped walnuts.

3. Add the egg and remaining 1/2 cup sugar substitute to a bowl and whisk until frothy.

4. Using a rubber spatula, fold the almond flour and salt into the frothy egg mixture and pour over the cranberries; spreading the mixture out to about 1/2 inch from the edge of the pie pan. (A 1/2 inch wide ring of cranberries around the edge of the dish should still be visible.) Bake for 40 to 45 minutes until top is golden brown, remove and let cool before slicing into 8 wedges. Serve warm topped with a scoop of quick and easy to make *"Faux" Vanilla Ice Cream,* recipe on the next page.

GEORGE'S TIPS:

Although this pie is great served warm or cold, when reheating be sure to use the oven and bake at 325 F for 20 minutes to keep a nice crispy topping!

172

calories 117
fat 12g
protein 1g
fiber 0g
net carbs 2

PREP TIME 15 MINS

COOK TIME 7 MINS

SERVES 4

desserts

FAUX VANILLA ICE CREAM

Desserts that are fast and easy are important so that you can "whip" them up when the urge strikes you! It was easy to re-invent ice cream but the challenge here was to create a low carb version without having to slave over a hot stove with eggs and cream for an hour and this recipe sure fills the bill!

shopping list

1 cup heavy cream
1/2 cup sugar substitute (recommended: Splenda)
1 teaspoon no sugar added vanilla extract
2 tablespoons whole milk ricotta cheese
SPECIAL EQUIPMENT: electric mixer

directions

1. With an electric mixer on high, whip the heavy cream in a bowl just until frothy and add in the sugar substitute, vanilla extract and ricotta cheese. Continue to whip on high until peaks form. Be careful not to over-whip, or cream will break.

2. Using a 3-ounce ice cream scoop, place 1 scoop each in a champagne glass and freeze as "faux" ice cream or serve refrigerated as a parfait.

 ## GEORGE'S TIPS:

Serve with fresh berries for the perfect presentation.

calories 233 | fat 20g | protein 9g | fiber 3g | net carbs 4

PREP TIME **15 MINS**

COOK TIME **25 MINS**

SERVES **9**

desserts

GINGERBREAD SQUARES WITH LEMON FROSTING

Whether it's for dessert or with coffee in the morning as you run out the door, this traditional treat is an all time comfort dessert that my Mom made for me when I was a kid. It was a favorite of mine then with the delicious thick lemon frosting that I would ceremoniously lick off the top before devouring the spicy cake! Today, I can still have my cake and eat it too!

directions

1. Preheat the oven to 350 degrees F. and spray the baking pan heavily with vegetable oil.

2. In a bowl whisk together the almond flour, milled flax seed, sugar substitute, baking powder, ginger, cinnamon and salt.

3. In another bowl, whisk the eggs, vanilla and soy milk until frothy. Combine the dry and wet ingredients and stir until combined.

4. Pour the batter into the prepared pan and spread evenly. Bake for about 25 minutes until golden brown and a toothpick comes out clean when stuck in the center. Cool completely before frosting with Lemon Frosting. Slice into 3 rows by 3 rows making 9 dessert portions or cut 5 by 5 to make 25 smaller party portions. Best served cold.

shopping list ✏

GINGERBREAD SQUARES
vegetable oil spray
1 1/2 cups almond flour
1/4 cup milled flax seed or flax seed meal
2/3 cup sugar substitute (recommended: Splenda)
1 1/2 teaspoons baking powder
1 1/2 teaspoons ground ginger
1 teaspoon ground cinnamon
1/4 teaspoon salt
4 large eggs
1 teaspoon vanilla extract (no sugar added)
1/4 cup unsweetened soy milk (may use heavy cream)
SPECIAL EQUIPMENT: 8 x 8 inch baking pan or dish
LEMON FROSTING
8 ounces cream cheese, softened
1/2 cup sugar substitute (recommended: Splenda)
2 tablespoons fresh lemon juice
1 teaspoon lemon zest

Lemon Frosting

1. Place all ingredients in a bowl and whisk until well blended.

 # GEORGE'S TIPS:

You may use egg whites or Eggbeaters in place of the whole eggs in the squares to cut down the fat. The cream cheese in the frosting may be substituted with a low fat or fat free version.

calories 138
fat 10g
protein 11g
fiber 2g

net carbs 3

PREP TIME **15 MINS**

COOK TIME **10 MINS**

SERVES **8**

desserts

MOCHA TOFU PARFAITS

I know what you're thinking, tofu as a dessert? Yes, absolutely! Silken tofu is a neutral flavor healthy alternative with the consistency of pudding or whipped cream that absorbs and becomes embodied by what is added to it. Therefore when flavored with bakers chocolate and sweetened with sugar substitute as in this recipe it tastes as good as or better than most chocolate mousse I have ever had or made!

shopping list ✏

1 batch **Chocolate Macadamia Bark**, recipe page: 171 (made without the macadamias)

1 tablespoon instant coffee, dissolved in 2 tablespoons hot water

1 tablespoon vanilla extract

4 cups silken tofu, (usually found in a 15 1/2 ounce package, buy 2)

1/4 cup sugar substitute (recommended: Splenda)

SPECIAL EQUIPMENT: food processor or blender and 8 parfait glasses

directions

1. Make the **Chocolate Macadamia Bark** without the macadamias; continue by adding the dissolved instant coffee and vanilla and mix until smooth.

2. Add the tofu, sugar substitute and chocolate mixture into a food processor and blend on medium speed for just a minute until smooth. Pour into parfait glasses and chill for at least 3 hours before serving.

GEORGE'S TIPS:

Serve topped with fresh strawberries or raspberries if desired.

PREP TIME	COOK TIME	SERVES	calories	fat	protein	fiber
35 MINS	0 MINS	4	330	33g	5g	0g

net carbs 3

desserts

FOOL PROOF CHEESECAKE ICE CREAM

Can you have too much cheesecake? I think not! When I snagged myself an ice cream maker, it was only a matter of time before I was churning up this new favorite. Cheesecake ice cream—I love it! So does Ben. And that other guy from Vermont.

shopping list

8 ounces cream cheese, softened and cut into 4pcs (may use low fat)

1 1/2 cups light cream (may use unsweetened soy milk)

1 1/2 teaspoon fresh squeezed lemon juice

1/4 cup sugar substitute (recommended: Splenda)

1 teaspoon vanilla extract

SPECIAL EQUIPMENT: food processor, any ice cream maker

directions

1. Place all ingredients into a food processor and blend for about 1 minute until smooth.

2. Pour mixture into an ice cream maker and turn for about 20 -30 minutes until thick and the motor slows.

3. Serve immediately in chilled dishes or store in the freezer as quickly as possible.

 GEORGE'S TIPS:

Homemade ice cream melts much quicker than store bought and after freezing you may need to let it thaw on the counter for 3 minutes or so to soften.

calories 100 | **fat 6g** | **protein 7g** | **net carbs 3** | **fiber 0g**

PREP TIME 10 MINS

COOK TIME 30 MINS

SERVES 4

desserts

SIMPLE QUICK CUSTARD

If you love Flan, then this is the ticket for you! With simple ingredients that are almost always at hand, you can make this classic dessert anytime! It's so easy to make, but tastes like you went to culinary school—or at least some kind of Flan making night course!

directions

1. Place the rack in the center position and preheat the oven to 375 degrees F. Spray the baking dishes with vegetable oil.

shopping list

vegetable oil spray

2 whole large eggs

2 large egg yolks only (save the whites for an omelet!)

1/2 cup sugar substitute (recommended: Splenda)

1 1/2 cups unsweetened soy milk, recommended: Silk brand (may use half and half)

1 tablespoon vanilla extract

SPECIAL EQUIPMENT: four 6 ounce Pyrex glass baking dishes.

2. Make a water bath so the custard cooks all the way through: Pour about 1 inch of water into a shallow roasting pan big enough to fit the 4 dishes and place it in the oven on the center rack to heat.

3. Add all the ingredients into a bowl and whisk until smooth. Use a rubber spatula and scrape batter into a large measuring cup.

4. Using the measuring cup pour equal amounts of the batter into each of the 4 dishes, filling them only about 2/3 full.

5. Place the filled dishes in the preheated water bath and bake for about 30 minutes or until a crust forms on top and the center feels firm to the touch. Remove from the oven and the water bath and let cool on the counter for 30 minutes followed by 2 hours in the refrigerator. Serve chilled with fresh blueberries and whipped cream if desired.

GEORGE'S TIPS:

Can't wait for them to chill? Try them warm!

calories 150
fat 12g
protein 7g
fiber 2g
net carbs 4

PREP TIME 10 MINS
COOK TIME 15 MINS
SERVES 10

desserts

RICOTTA CARNIVAL FRITTERS

Who doesn't remember going to the carnival and drooling over the intoxicating smell of Elephant Ears or Fried Dough? You couldn't help but follow your nose only to see them being made and then laid out in front of you blanketed with an addicting glow of white confectioners' sugar and others better yet smothered in tempting toppings from jams to fudge! We're talkin' real American comfort food here!

shopping list

2 cups canola oil

1 cup soy flour (recommend: Arrowhead Mills brand)

1/2 cup sugar substitute (recommend: Splenda)

1 tablespoon baking powder

1 cup whole milk ricotta cheese

3 large eggs

SPECIAL EQUIPMENT: portable deep-fryer recommended, sheet pan with paper towels.

directions

1. Fill and preheat a portable deep fryer to 350* F or place a heavy pot over medium-high heat with at least an inch of vegetable oil. Heat the oil to 350* F; it is important to monitor and maintain the temperature or the fritters will burn before the inside is cooked. (Never overfill the fryer or pot with oil. You must leave room for it to bubble up when the fritters are added.)

2. In a medium bowl, combine the soy flour, all but 1 tablespoon of the sugar substitute and the baking powder. (1 tablespoon sugar substitute is reserved for dusting the cooked fritters.)

3. Next add the ricotta and eggs and mix well with a rubber spatula.

4. Using 2 regular tablespoons and working quickly, carefully drop scant tablespoons of the batter into the hot oil using one spoon to scrape the batter off the other. Stop putting more into the oil when the first ones start to brown. Once they are a dark golden brown on the bottom side use a slotted metal spoon to turn each fritter over and continue to cook until dark golden brown on that side. Remove with the slotted spoon and drain on the paper lined sheet pan. Repeat process for remaining batter.

5. While hot, sprinkle the fritters with the reserved sugar substitute and serve. Fritters may also be served cold the same day, but do not refrigerate.

GEORGE'S TIPS:

Try filling these fritters with fresh whipped cream (made without sugar, of course) to make little cream puffs! Or stuff them with just a tad of sugar free all natural jelly for delightfully decadent mini jelly donuts!!!

calories 90 | fat 7g | protein 3g | fiber 1g | net carbs **3**

PREP TIME **15 MINS**

COOK TIME **10 MINS**

SERVES **12**

desserts

HOLIDAY ALMOND COOKIES

These scrumptiously great morsels remind me of butter cookies and sugar cookies combined! Need I say anything else? Once you try one you will scream for MORE, almost frighteningly loud. They make great Holiday gifts too; that is if they make it out of your kitchen before everybody eats them all!

directions

1. Add the eggs to a bowl and whisk until frothy.

2. Then add the food coloring and sugar substitute and blend.

3. Next add the almond flour, salt and butter and mix well with a wooden spoon.

shopping list

2 large eggs, room temperature

20 drops red or green food coloring (optional)

1 cup sugar substitute (recommended: Splenda)

1 1/2 cups almond flour, ground from blanched almonds

1/8 teaspoon salt (pinch)

1 tablespoon butter softened to room temperature (May use trans-fat free margarine)

24 pieces almond slices

4. Place soft mixture on a 12 inch length sheet of Saran wrap and roll up like a burrito into a log about 8" long and twist the ends of the Saran wrap to close. Refrigerate overnight or freeze for about 1 hour until firm. (You can reshape the log after about 45 minutes of chilling into a more round shape if needed.)

5. Preheat oven to 375°F and line a sheet pan with parchment paper or a silicone mat.

6. Remove log from refrigerator or freezer and unwrap the Saran wrap. The dough will be very sticky so be sure to use a thin, sharp knife and work quickly to slice the dough into 24 even pieces with a constant back and forth slicing motion and place them evenly spaced on a sheet pan. (If they get out of shape just press them back into shape on the cookie sheet with your fingers.)

7. Top each raw cookie with a single almond slice, pressing it down about half way with your finger to make it stick and bake for 10 minutes until golden brown. Cool and serve or store on the counter in a covered container for up to 3 days.

GEORGE'S TIPS:

Be sure to bring a batch of these with you to all of your family gatherings this Holiday season so you'll be sure to have a treat of your own. Fill up an old Christmas tin or jar and give these as a gift!

PREP TIME **5 MINS**

COOK TIME **0 MINS**

SERVES **8**

calories **40** · fat **0g** · protein **3g** · fiber **1g**

net carbs **5**

INSTANT STRAWBERRY ICE CREAM

We created this recipe late one night while watching a movie and craving something sweet. We never expected it to come out so good! The ice cold strawberries instantly freeze the whole dessert, leaving you without any necessary freezer time, which is always a good thing when your movie is still playing in the other room!

shopping list

2 cups frozen strawberries

1 cup fat free ricotta Cheese

1/4 cup sugar substitute (recommended: Splenda)

1 tablespoon no sugar added vanilla extract

SPECIAL EQUIPMENT: food processor

directions

1. If your strawberries are large you may want to cut them in half before freezing.

2. Place all of the ingredients into your food processor. Blend for about 2 minutes or until silky smooth.

3. Serve immediately in a fancy glass with a sprig of fresh mint if desired.

 ## GEORGE'S TIPS:

Buy lots of extra strawberries whenever they are in season or on sale and keep the extras in the freezer for this recipe or smoothies whenever you want.

fat **27g** protein **14g**

calories **318** fiber **0g**

net carbs **6**

PREP TIME **15 MINS**

COOK TIME **55 MINS**

SERVES **8**

desserts

STELLA STYLE NY CHEESECAKE MINIS

Rachel's world famous cheesecake takes a bit of effort and time and it's well worth it, but this new quicker and easier version was developed for those of you like me who just want to get dessert MADE already! These delightful mini cheesecakes are now a staple in our Stella Style arsenal of comforting cravings busters and we know they will be for you too!

directions

1. Place the rack in the center position and preheat the oven to 350 degrees F. Spray the 8 baking dishes with vegetable oil.

2. Make a water bath so the cheesecake cups cook all the way through: Pour about 1 inch of water into a shallow roasting pan big enough to fit the 8 dishes and place it in the oven on the center rack to heat. (Use 2 pans if needed.)

3. Add all the ingredients into a food processor and blend on medium speed for just a minute until smooth. Use a rubber spatula and scrape batter into a large measuring cup.

4. Using the measuring cup pour equal amounts of the batter into each of the 8 dishes, filling them only about 3/4 full. (If there isn't enough batter just make 1 less, it happens!)

5. Place the filled cups in the preheated water bath and bake for about 55 minutes or until cheesecakes are golden brown on top. Remove from the oven and the water bath and let cool on the counter for 30 minutes followed by 3 hours in the refrigerator.

shopping list

vegetable oil spray
16 ounces cream cheese, softened
2 cups ricotta cheese
2 whole large eggs
1 large egg yolk
1 cup sugar substitute, granulated in bag variety (recommended: Splenda)
1/2 cup unsweetened soy milk (recommended: Silk brand, but may use half and half)
1 tablespoon vanilla extract
1 tablespoon fresh lemon juice
SPECIAL EQUIPMENT: food processor and eight 6 ounce Pyrex glass baking dishes (May use aluminum throw away variety available in the baking isle at grocery stores)

GEORGE'S TIPS:

Serve garnished with fresh sliced strawberries and blueberries if desired.

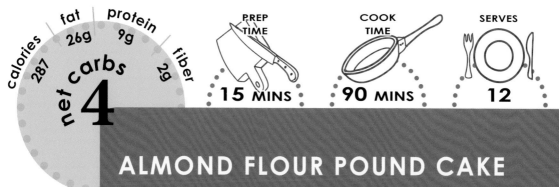

calories 287 | fat 26g | protein 9g | fiber 2g | net carbs **4**

PREP TIME **15 MINS** | COOK TIME **90 MINS** | SERVES **12**

desserts

ALMOND FLOUR POUND CAKE

Pound cake is usually made with a full pound of butter but when you use almonds you don't need all that butter as the almonds provide good monounsaturated fats that keep the cake moist and delicious! Since the almonds are also taking the place of the white flour in this recipe you get double the benefits! With no added sugar, no flour and added good fats you can indulge in this classic cake without the classic guilt!

directions

1. Place the rack in the center of the oven and preheat oven to 300 degrees F.

2. In a bowl mix together the almond flour, sugar substitute, baking powder and salt.

shopping list

2 1/2 cups almond flour, ground from blanched almonds

1 1/2 cups sugar substitute, granulated in bag variety (recommended: Splenda)

1 1/2 teaspoons baking powder

1 1/2 teaspoons salt

7 large eggs

3/4 cup trans-fat free margarine (recommended: Smart Balance)

6 ounces cream cheese, softened

1 1/2 teaspoons vanilla extract

1 1/2 teaspoons fresh lemon juice

SPECIAL EQUIPMENT: mixer and 9 x 5 inch loaf pan, bottom lined with parchment paper and sprayed with vegetable oil

3. In another bowl beat the eggs and set aside.

4. With an electric mixer on high speed whip the butter and cream cheese. Add the vanilla, lemon juice and beaten eggs and blend until smooth; about 1 minute more.

5. Combine the dry and wet ingredients together and mix well. Pour the batter into the prepared pan and bake until the top starts to become lightly golden brown and a toothpick stuck in the center comes out clean, about 1 1/2 hours. Cool before removing from pan and slice into 6 thick pieces and then cut each slice in half to make 12 portions. Serve warm or cold.

GEORGE'S TIPS:

This pound cake works perfect for making strawberry shortcakes!

PREP TIME

COOK TIME

SERVES

calories | fat | protein | fiber

net carbs

shopping list ✏️

directions

calories

fat

protein

net carbs

fiber

PREP TIME

COOK TIME

SERVES

shopping list

directions

 PREP TIME

 COOK TIME

 SERVES

calories

fat

protein

fiber

net carbs

my recipes

shopping list

directions

calories | fat | protein | fiber

net carbs

PREP TIME

COOK TIME

SERVES

shopping list

directions

PREP TIME

COOK TIME

SERVES

calories fat protein fiber

net carbs

shopping list

directions

calories | fat | protein | fiber

net carbs

PREP TIME

COOK TIME

SERVES

shopping list

directions

about the authors

George Stella, a professional chef for twenty five years, is an official spokesman for the Junior Leagues' *Kids in the Kitchen* initiative to empower youth to make healthy lifestyle choices. He has appeared on numerous television and news shows, including two seasons of his own show, *Low Carb and Lovin' It* on the Food Network. He has written two previous cookbooks, *George Stella's Livin' Low Carb* and *Eating Stella Style*. Currently, he is executive chef of the Havana Country Club Restaurant in The Villages, Florida. Connecticut born, he's spent more than half of his life in Florida, where he lives today with his wife Rachel.

Christian Stella's fiction has been published in *Look-Look* and *Facets Literary Magazine*, where it was nominated for The Pushcart Prize. He has coauthored one previous cookbook with his father, *Eating Stella Style*. He lives in Orlando, Florida, with his wife Elise, who did the illustrations for this book.

about the book

The nutritional information and calorie counts on the recipes in this book were compiled from reputable sources to the best of our ability. Counts may differ, depending on the specific brands of ingredients you purchase. Carbohydrate counts especially differ from brand to brand, so always read the label! If healthier substitutions are suggested in a recipe, the nutritional data was compiled from the first ingredient, not the substitution.

Net carbohydrate counts shown in this book were figured by subtracting fiber grams from the total carbohydrate count, as the fiber does not absorb into the body. Fiber carbs are the ONLY type that we subtract. Net carbs were rounded to the nearest .5 of a gram.

Sugar substitute measurements in this book refer to "bulk" sugar substitute that comes in large boxes or bags, not single serving packets. "Bulk" sugar substitute retains the same measurements as real sugar, while packets are far more concentrated and do not measure correctly.

All food photographs were taken in the Stella home, with food cooked and plated by George and Rachel. We put an emphasis on taking photographs of real food, prepared by the recipe directions, rather than "faking it" to look good for the camera. The food was then devoured. Lighting for all photographs provided by the Florida sun.

Recipes